TRANIFESTO

TRANIFESTO

*Selected Columns and
Other Ramblings from a
Transgendered Mind*

To Spring –
You're beautiful
& fun – just like
a breath of
Spring –
Matt
Kailey

Matt Kailey

To order additional copies of this book, contact:
Xlibris Corporation
1-888-795-4274
www.Xlibris.com
Orders@Xlibris.com
15740

CONTENTS

For Sean Gardner (my savior), Ian Philips (my hero) and
Rod and Shirley Kailey (my late, great parents).
Thanks to Kathy W., Robynne Pennington and T-esign,
Carolee Laughton, Jessie Shafer, Susan Condor,
Rachael St. Claire, Bonnie Zare, Sharon Benson,
Christopher Leach, Kevin and Don, Keith Lucero,
The Gender Identity Center of Colorado and
anyone else who I have forgotten.

TRANS-LATIONS

The transgendered community has created a language of its own, since none was previously available to help us describe our experience. If you ask five trans people the meaning of a specific term, you will often get five different answers. The following definitions are generally accepted in the transgendered community. However, some definitions vary among certain people or groups. They are presented here to help the non-trans reader understand my language and some of the references in the book and to make the trans reader aware of the meanings that I ascribe to the terms. Since the definitions can get rather clinical (i.e. boring), the reader might want to skim them and refer back if a certain definition is needed.

Binary Gender System: Refers to the two-gendered (masculine and feminine) system that exists in most cultures and that is based largely on genitalia.

Bio-male/bio-female, natal male/natal female, genetic male/genetic female: These terms are often used to describe men who were born men and women who were born women, as opposed to people who have transitioned into a male or female body and identification. A preferred term among many trans people is "non-trans male" or "non-trans female."

Chest Surgery/Top Surgery: Refers to the surgical reconstruction of the chest for transmen to create a male chest and can involve liposuction or a mastectomy, with or without nipple reconstruction.

Crossdresser: Refers to a person who dresses in clothing of the opposite sex, usually for the purposes of relieving gender discomfort. In the past, this term has been used synonymously with "transvestite," which has taken on negative connotations and is not often used in the TG community. Crossdressers are not drag queens. Drag queens are men who dress as women for stage performance. Drag kings are the female counterparts of drag queens. Some people who choose to perform drag might be transgendered, but, in this author's opinion, performing drag does not mean a person is transgendered. Many in the gender community disagree with this author on this point.

Female-to-Male (FtM): Refers to an individual assigned female at birth who identifies as male, either full or part-time, and often dresses as male and assumes a male role in society. More specifically, refers to a natal female who undergoes gender reassignment to male. Many natal females who have undergone such reassignment prefer the term "transman" or "man."

Gender: This term is often used synonymously with sex, but it is actually more of a social construct, whereas sex is physical and biological. Gender defines roles, behaviors and identity apart from physical sex characteristics. There is arguably a biological component to gender.

Gender Dysphoria: The feeling of being at odds with one's body, genitalia, birth sex and/or society's expectations of the roles and behaviors that coincide with the birth label of male or female. Many feel that this term carries a negative connotation as it suggests a psychological, rather than a physiological, basis for transgenderism. Gender Identity Disorder, a psychological diagnosis that appears in the *DSM* (the *Diagnostic and Statistical Manual* used by therapists to diagnose certain mental illnesses), is also disputed by many who believe that transgenderism is a medical condition, or that it is not a "condition" at all but simply a way of being.

Gender Identity: The internal feelings and identification that individuals have with regard to being male or female. Gender identity includes how individuals feel about their physical bodies and their societal roles, expectations and behaviors. Most people feel comfortable with their birth sex and the gender identification and most of the societal roles that go with it. Some people have a gender identity at odds with their bodies and the roles and behaviors that are expected of them.

Gender Presentation: The externalization of gender identity—clothing, hairstyles, hobbies, interests, behaviors, mannerisms and other visible expressions of one's gender.

Gender Reassignment, Sex Reassignment, Sex Change: To correct the physical sex, through hormones, surgery or both, to adhere to an individual's gender identity. Individuals who undergo these procedures are often referred to as transsexuals, although some reject that label and feel that once the procedures are complete and all identification papers are changed, they are members of the sex opposite of their birth sex.

Gender Transition: Refers to the process of moving from one gender to another through the use of hormones, surgery or both and includes such things as legal name change, change in identification papers and change in clothing, appearance, mannerisms and other identifying gender markers.

Gender Variant: Used to describe appearance, behavior or both that does not conform to accepted societal norms regarding male and female appearance and/or behavior.

GLB: Initials used to refer to the gay, lesbian and bisexual community.

Hir: A gender-neutral pronoun that is a combination of "his" and "her." Other gender-neutral pronouns include "nu" and "zie."

Intersexed: Refers to those who, at birth, exhibit some physical characteristics of both sexes or have ambiguous genitalia or differing chromosomal structures. When the genitalia of a newborn does not conform to the standard "male" and "female" genitalia most often seen, doctors and/ or parents often choose (sometimes incorrectly) the sex to assign and surgical procedures are initiated to correct the "problem." A movement is currently underway by adults who were born intersexed to leave intersexed children as born and allow these individuals to choose gender assignment and surgical procedures, if desired, at a later stage in life. Intersexed people are not necessarily transgendered, in the opinion of this author, although they might be if the sex chosen for them at birth is not the sex they are comfortable with in life. Many in the gender community disagree with this author on this point and intersexed people are often listed as part of the transgender community.

Male-to-Female (MtF): Refers to an individual assigned male at birth who identifies as female, either full or part-time, and often dresses as female and assumes a female role in society. More specifically, refers to a natal male who undergoes gender reassignment to female. Many natal males who have undergone such reassignment prefer the term "transwoman" or "woman."

Non-trans male/female: See Bio-male/female

Phalloplasty: Refers to the operation used to surgically construct a penis for transmen.

Sex, Sex Assignment, Anatomical Sex, Birth Sex, Natal Sex: Refers to the label of male or female given at birth and based on genitalia. The labels of male and female throughout life are based on primary and secondary physical sex characteristics and carry wide-ranging implications for their owners.

Sexual Orientation: Refers to the sex and gender to which an individual is physically and emotionally attracted. This is not the same thing as gender identity, which refers to the sex and gender that an individual feels he or she is inside.

T: This letter has two distinct meanings in the trans community. It is used to designate the trans community as a whole, as in GLBT (gay, lesbian, bisexual and transgender community), and it is also used among transmen when referring to testosterone.

Transgender(ed) (TG): Most generally used as an umbrella term that encompasses a range of people. In general usage, it can refer to anyone who transgresses gender norms. More specifically, it is used to refer to people who experience discomfort and/or unhappiness, either some or all of the time, with their birth sex, including their anatomy, appearance and expected social roles. The discomfort can be expressed in activities such as adopting the behavior and dress of the opposite sex, either full or part-time, living in the role of the opposite sex, either full or part-time, or in physically altering the body through hormones and/or surgery (see Gender Reassignment and Transsexual). It can also refer to those who present as androgynous or do not define themselves by gender at all. In some cases, these people self-identify as "genderqueer," "genderless" or "neutrois."

Transman/woman: See Female-to-Male and Male-to-Female

Transsexual, Transexual (TS): Most commonly used to refer to an individual who has undergone gender reassignment that includes surgery and/or hormones, name change, change of birth certificate and change of identifying papers, such as social security cards, diplomas, transcripts, passports, etc. These individuals have experienced such discomfort with their birth sex that many believe this is a life-saving procedure. Some use this term to refer to an individual who is living full-time as a member of the opposite sex but has had no surgical or hormonal intervention.

INTRODUCTION:
ARE YOU DONE?

I started my gender transition from female to male in 1997 and began writing a column for *The Gender Identity Center of Colorado Journal* shortly thereafter. With the column, *my point eXactlY*, as my vehicle, I was able to chronicle my feelings and experiences throughout my transition. In the pages that follow, the reader will find a selection of my columns and other essays, as well as an explanation of the issues and events that prompted these outbursts of the pen (or the keyboard). Some topics can be generalized to both female-to-male and male-to-female transsexuals. Others are specific to the female-to-male, a role in which I have had all my experience. The selections are not presented in chronological order but are grouped in a way that I hope will allow the reader, especially the non-trans reader, to understand the mysteries of gender transition. I have included a Frequently Asked Questions section with more information for the non-trans reader.

Clinically speaking, gender transition can be a little boring (imagine that). It consists of therapy, the administration of hormones and the unpleasantness of various surgeries, all intended to change the outward appearance of the recipient, trans-porting him or her into the gender of comfort or the "opposite" gender. Physical transition does not happen overnight or over the course of a weekend. Some non-trans people assume that a female enters a hospital on Friday night and emerges Monday morning as a fully developed and fully functional adult male. I wish I knew where that hospital was. Although some of the physical changes brought on by testosterone are irreversible, such as facial and body hair and elongated vocal cords, it must be taken for a lifetime to maintain a male pattern of body fat distribution and male muscle development. Chest surgery does occur in a few hours, with a varying recovery time, but certain genital surgeries require several trips to the hospital over a period of several months or years, depending on finances and complications. And most transmen opt for a hysterectomy, if possible.

Transition is a process, not a product, and spans a period of time that is usually decided by a transsexual's desires and bank account. A question I am frequently asked when I "come out" as a transsexual is, "Are you done?" As if I were a Thanksgiving turkey, the assumption is that there is a specific ending date when the little bell on the timer dings and I can then proclaim to the world that I am male. Most people who ask this question believe that transition ends with genital surgery and that no one is "done" until this is complete. There are even some laws that use genital surgery as a marker of a completed transition. In reality, "done" has more to do with the person undergoing a transition than it does with a specific time frame or set of circumstances. Some transsexual people never have surgery and are satisfied with the results of hormones alone. Others opt only for certain surgeries, such as chest reconstruction, but reject others, such as genital surgery.

There are many reasons why a transsexual might not undergo every medical option available. Some surgeries are very expensive and, since insurance, at least in the United States, rarely covers any part of a transition, are simply not affordable. Some people do not want to undergo multiple surgeries because of the risks or the pain involved. Certain health conditions prevent the taking of hormones. And, although there are transsexual people who feel that they will never be "whole" unless the body has been completely changed, there are others who don't feel the need to be what our culture considers "totally male" or "totally female." The feeling of "doneness" that exists in any transsexual's mind might be completely at odds with what a non-trans person considers a finished product.

And physical changes are only part of a transition. They do not prepare a person to function adequately in a gender in which he or she was not socialized. Socialization is often a massive barrier that is difficult to overcome. In some cases, a transsexual person must literally be taught how to function in his or her "new" gender—how to walk, talk, sit, stand and interact with others as a member of that gender, things that were learned by non-trans people in childhood and adolescence. Some trans people spend a great deal of time learning these new behaviors, while to others they come naturally. Then there are some who are simply unconcerned with how "male" or "female" they appear in their new roles.

Comfort with one's body and a congruity between body and mind are the goals of transition and these concepts mean different things to different people. For some, a mixture of the masculine and feminine body types, behaviors and thought processes is sufficient. For others, only a complete and all-inclusive transition to the "opposite" gender will do.

I use quotations with the term "opposite" because I believe that we create many problems for ourselves in referring to each other (men to women and women to men) as "opposites."

First of all, when we use the term, we are automatically setting up a strict binary gender system (a two-gendered system) that leaves no room for anyone who does not specifically conform, physically and emotionally, to either "male" or "female." The Intersex Society of North America presents on its website the statistic that one in every one hundred people, at birth, has a body that differs from the standard male or female body in some way. These differences are not always obvious and do not necessarily interfere with living in a binary gender system, but might have serious implications when talk turns to chromosome testing for marriage licenses or how many inches make an "acceptable" (in other words, "male") penis. If we have only "opposite" genders, where is the place for every one out of one hundred people who are born with some type of intersexed condition? And this does not even take into account the thousands of people with transsexual bodies, bodies that have been altered by hormones, surgery or both.

Another reason that the use of "opposite" is problematic is that major, even irreconcilable, incompatibility is inherent in the term. We have already been told that men and women are from different planets. It is a wonder that the two "opposite" genders can communicate at all. If two people are opposite, it is likely to mean that they have nothing in common, yet our society expects them to marry, raise children and go about life together—and this arrangement is considered the norm. "Opposite" focuses on people's differences, not their similarities, and the failure of male/female relationships can be the result.

The term also establishes polarity, with no room to move between genders, to adopt characteristics of both male and female genders or to identify as something else entirely. There is little room to maneuver in such a state of opposites and even non-transgendered people often have trouble subscribing to all the roles and expectations that are assigned to their gender. However, the pressure to do so is immense, since to diverge puts a person at odds with, or "opposite" of, him or herself and the rest of society.

But the term is firmly embedded in our culture. Like a pesky houseguest, it has made itself quite at home and shows no signs of leaving (or cleaning up the bathroom). I even use it, to my own chagrin, because it is easy, understood by all and it allows me to get my point across—*my point eXactlY*, which is where we came in.

I underwent a gender transition and lived to tell about it (most of us live, fewer of us tell about it). I take male hormones (pharmaceutical testosterone) by intramuscular injection, and will take them for the rest of my life. I have had chest surgery. I have legally changed my name and my driver's license. I have lived in society as a female and as a male (and, for a very brief time in early transition, as something no one could seem to identify), and there is not as much difference as people who have lived only as one or the other might think.

Certainly, I have noticed differences. As a female, I was afraid to walk after dark and, when I had to, I was quite aware of who was behind me, in front of me and on either side, as well as which houses had porch lights on and where I might find safe refuge if necessary. Now, after transition, I rarely worry. I am, however, more likely to get shot, more likely to be involved in a physical fight and more likely to be expected to intervene in someone else's fight. I am also now expected to be able to lift heavy objects and change my own flat tires. Other men speak to me in a way, and with language, that they never did when I was female. I am told I have male privilege, but I was never socialized to expect it and wouldn't know what it was if it was handed to me wrapped in a big blue bow. But I also know now that men feel the same insecurities that women do, that men and women have many of the same needs and wants and that, if people in general were taught to open up to each other, we would probably, for the most part, get along just dandy.

I have had so many interesting experiences during my transition that I regret not keeping a journal. But, in a way, my column was and is my journal—it reflects much of what was going on with me at any given time in the process. It became so popular that I decided to publish this compilation, which, hopefully, will not only take the reader along on parts of my journey, but will allow the reader a journey of his, her or hir own.

CHAPTER ONE

TEXTBOOK TRANSSEXUALS

I am not a textbook transsexual. In fact, my life experience defies almost everything ever written *about* transsexuals by non-transsexuals. Unfortunately, that body of information comprises most of the reference material to which doctors and therapists refer when diagnosing and working with trans people. The *DSM*, the *Diagnostic and Statistical Manual* that is used by mental health professionals to assign labels to people who display behaviors and thought patterns considered to be "abnormal" in polite society, is filled with inaccurate information on transgendered folk, especially in reference to female-to-males. It is frightening to think of the transgendered females who are being misdiagnosed and mistreated at the hands of inexperienced therapists who use the *DSM* as their diagnostic bible. I was lucky enough to encounter a therapist who had such an extensive knowledge of trans issues that she had no need to consult the dreaded manual to determine what I would need. I was not a tomboy, which is one of the first clues therapists look for in diagnosing a gender identity disorder in natal females. I was also not attracted to females, a significant precursor to a *DSM* diagnosis. In fact, if my therapist had followed the narrow guidelines set forth in that manual, I would not be writing this today.

That the *DSM* provides erroneous diagnostic tools for professionals working with trans people is only a symptom of a larger problem—the notion that varying gender identification is a cause for concern at all. Our culture maintains a strict binary system that identifies only two genders—masculine and feminine—and aligns those two genders with specific genitalia. Any person who deviates from the behaviors, appearance and roles that were designated to that individual by way of his or her genitalia is considered to have a mental health issue. Any person who chooses (and some would say that it is not a choice) to deal with that incongruity by undergoing gender reassignment is subject to a strict, time-lined regulation of his or her decisions and actions. The *Harry Benjamin Standards of Care* is a document created by the Harry Benjamin Association that lays out specific, step-by-step procedures defining how transgendered people wishing to make a gender transition are to be "managed" by the psychiatric and medical professionals who deal with them. These standards include distinct time frames for beginning hormones and having surgery and spell out particular actions that trans people must take before being "allowed" to transition. The *Standards of Care* has been heralded by some and criticized by others. I have my own opinions.

SLEEPING WITH HARRY BENJAMIN: THE IMBALANCE OF POWER IN THE TRANSGENDER THERAPEUTIC RELATIONSHIP

Imagine that you have a fatal disease. The disease is difficult to detect and can take many forms. It is not visible to anyone looking at you and medical tests to diagnose it are not always reliable. But you have all the symptoms and you are fading fast. You don't have much time left. Now imagine that someone has a pill that will cure you. In order to get that pill, you must prove to the person holding it that you have the disease. He or she can't see it. There are no blood tests or x-rays to confirm it. Only you can convince this person that you have it. What are you going to say? Probably anything that you think this person wants to hear. Will you lie to get the pill? Maybe, if you believe that it will save your life. Will you say things that might show inconsistencies between what you are experiencing and the textbook course of the illness? Probably not, if you are worried about casting doubt in that person's mind. After all, this pill can mean the difference between life and death. In the relationship between you and the person holding the pill, who has the power? Here's a hint—it ain't you, babe.

I work in the child welfare field. In many cases, my agency takes custody of people's children and places them in foster care until their parents resolve whatever issues led them to endanger their children. In these cases, the court often orders therapy. Many therapists refuse to work with families who have been court ordered to see them. These therapists know that therapy rarely produces tangible results unless the patient recognizes a need for help. Force doesn't work. They also know that parents who are system-savvy can and will say exactly what they need to say in order to get their children home. The therapy is a game. And the therapist, whose report is ultimately a strong deciding factor in the children's return to the family, owns all the property on the Monopoly board. Some therapists don't like to play this way.

The same is true with therapists who work with the transgendered under the sometimes-stifling *Harry Benjamin Standards of Care*. The therapist has something the patient wants very much. In fact, the patient's life may depend on it. The therapist controls the patient's access to hormones and surgery. The patient must say and do exactly what the therapist wants in order to receive the life-sustaining gifts that the therapist has to bestow. The patient must watch his or her step—if the wrong thing is said, if the therapist is angered, if a reasonable doubt is implanted, the letter approving hormones or surgery, more valuable than the Holy Grail, could be withheld, delayed or refused altogether. This is therapy? If the patient must weigh every word, withhold any information that could be taken as doubt, fear or indecisiveness, how can he or she possibly be helped? A therapeutic relationship must be built on honesty and trust. But does the patient dare to be honest when that honesty could lead the therapist to question whether or not transition is indicated? The therapist holds all the cards. How therapeutically beneficial is this imbalance of power to those who truly need help?

Recently, a therapist, the mother of young children, was killed in her office in California. There are different versions of what actually took place but, whether the shooting was accidental or deliberate, it shouldn't have happened. It was the outgrowth of the imbalance of power. It was no different from a street robbery, in which the victim has something (usually money) that the perpetrator wants or needs. The gun goes off, intentionally or accidentally, and an innocent person dies for possessing a desired object. And the thief, whose motivation often remains unknown, will go to prison for the rest of his (or her) life. Two lives lost, needlessly. There is danger in this type of relationship, for both sides, and the *Standards of Care* perpetuates the precarious situation.

I do not propose that people receive hormones or surgery on demand. I am not in favor of anyone being able to walk into a clinic off the street and walk out (or be wheeled out) several hours later sans breasts or penis. I don't want to walk into my doctor's office with a side ache, say that I think I have appendicitis and wind up on an operating table when I really just needed an antacid tablet.

A person requesting gender reassignment must be

evaluated, a history must be gathered, other causes of the presenting gender issues must be ruled out. But once those other causes are eliminated, once it has been determined that the person is of sound mind and body and knows what he or she needs, there should be no delay in getting the necessary treatment.

The *Standards of Care* discounts the ability of the patient to determine his/her needs. It infantilizes the patient and awards the therapist more power than he/she may even want. It sets up a dangerous imbalance of power that nullifies a true therapeutic relationship that could benefit the patient in untold ways. It puts up a wall between the therapist and the patient that is damaging to both.

We must take back the power that is ours—the right to make our own decisions, as adults, about our own bodies, minds and souls. A relationship with a good therapist can be extremely rewarding and beneficial. To have someone to communicate with, in total honesty, who is not there to judge but to help, can mean the difference between just existing and living a full, meaningful and complete life. The *Standards of Care* does not always allow this for the transgendered person. And that is truly a tragedy for both the therapist and the patient.

A primary concern with the *DSM* and the *Standards of Care* is that these documents focus on transgenderism as a psychological condition. In fact, no cause for body/mind gender disagreement has been determined. It could be psychological, physiological, a little of both or simply another way of being human in the ongoing epic mystery known as life. Whatever the cause, gender identity is not a choice, just as sexual orientation is not a choice. Many believe that transitioning is also not a choice. If the incongruity between a person's gender identity and his or her body and social roles is strong enough, he or she will transition or die.

Although quite a few transgendered individuals are able to remain in their birth sex and live part-time in the gender with which they identify, or ignore gender designations altogether, many are not. A large number of transgendered suicides occur because people are not able to transition, for whatever reason—marriage, children, employment, finances, community and so on.

Gender reassignment is not socially accepted in our culture and is not covered by insurance. The costs are nearly prohibitive for the average transgendered taxpaying citizen. Minorities, who experience other prejudices as well and who are often in underpaid jobs, find it especially difficult. And our culture finds transsexuals so morally reprehensible that we, as a society, seem to prefer death (by suicide) for these individuals to appropriate medical treatment. Also, because there is such shame in our culture around anyone who deviates from the standard male/female heterosexual identifications, it is difficult for transgendered people, especially those from rural areas and small towns, to find support and information. The Internet has helped with this, but it is much more beneficial to connect face-to-face with others.

In the past twenty to thirty years, a handful of gender centers in larger metropolitan areas have had the daunting task of servicing whatever trans individuals could gain access to them. These services have focused primarily on emotional support and on providing information. Until very recently, trans people who transitioned did so in secrecy and were urged to start new lives in their new gender and remain "in the closet" about their transness, to spare them from humiliation, assault and even death at the hands of others who did not approve. There is, however, a trans movement underway that is becoming more and more visible and is focusing on politics rather than support, on being "out" and being heard, on changing attitudes and legislation. Those trans people who are "out" are demanding rights that were previously unheard of and are making names for themselves in the larger community. Unfortunately, those few in the spotlight cannot do it all, and the shame and danger of being a transsexual remain. In this Catch-22 situation, transsexuals will not be safe "coming out" until popular attitude changes and popular attitude will not change until more and more transsexuals come out and are heard.

Attitudes toward gay men and lesbians are, too slowly, changing as people increasingly realize that they know (and like) someone—a neighbor, coworker or relative—who is gay or lesbian. When more and more people begin to realize that they also know (and like) a trans person, we will hopefully see a positive paradigm shift. We are still waiting.

CHAPTER TWO

TRANS IDENTITY

Going through a gender transition is a bit like being born, without the scary doctors and the disorienting, headfirst trip down a suffocating tunnel. You can literally start your life over, no matter what your age, and make those important decisions that someone else made for you when you started the original trip decades ago. You are old enough to reject the idea of handing out pink or blue bubble gum cigars emblazoned with "It's a Boy" or "It's a Girl" in favor of serving the strongest liquor available at your coming-out party. You can pass on the pacifiers and satisfy your oral cravings in whatever way you choose (I stayed with cigarettes—food ranks right up there). You can skip the stifling piano lessons that your mother hoped would turn you into a toddling child prodigy in favor of the hobby that you have always dreamed about but that might have given you away (pro-wrestling or needlepoint, depending on your original gender).

And, best of all, you get to choose your own name. No longer do you need to be saddled with the moniker of your mother's favorite soap opera character. Never again will signing on the dotted line remind you of the promise that your father made on his great-uncle Herman's deathbed. (If there's a transman out there named Herman, first, let me apologize. Second, let me ask, "What the hell were you thinking?") Now you can choose the name of your own most admired television star or your favorite dead relative. I chose the name my parents planned to give me at birth had I been born a boy the first time around. It's not my favorite name, but the problem with favorite names is that they tend to change when one soap character dies and is replaced by a sexier, better looking or smarter one. My name is a name that should have been and that's what makes it right.

Choosing a name is one of the earliest steps in gender transition and is the beginning of a new identity-formation. But it is definitely only the beginning. For the first year or two of my transition, I struggled with an identity crisis that seemed to eclipse the original gender conflict that brought me to that place to begin with. Male hormones were morphing my body into someone unrecognizable (more about that later), but my psyche still said I was me, whoever that was, and the "whoever that was" turned out to be the biggest problem. In the beginning, the face in the mirror was still that of a female, albeit a masculine one, and the breasts, though tied down, were still there. Although the clothing was purchased in the men's department, the body it covered was decidedly womanly. As testosterone took hold, the voice crackled like a static-filled radio, the muscles of the upper body swelled and the face in the mirror began to take on hard edges and sprout hair, but the question remained the same—"Who is that?"

We are a society of labels and I was having a hard time finding one that fit. Was I a man? A transman? A female-to-male transsexual? All or none of the above? My life was turning into a multiple choice exam. There were so many designer labels at my disposal that I felt as if I'd taken a wrong turn and entered Saks instead of Target. It took me a while to decide, but now, several years later, I still use the label I selected in the beginning. What's in a name? Everything.

WHAT DO YOU CALL YOURSELF?

"Hi, I'm Matt and I'm a transman." No, these are not my opening remarks at a 12-step group, nor is this my typical introduction at social gatherings. It is, however, the way I self-identify and the words I might use to explain my curious appearance to anyone with the chutzpa to ask. We all have certain words or phrases that we use to describe ourselves—gay, straight, transsexual, transgendered, liberal, conservative, in need of serious intervention, whatever. Many FtMs prefer to identify as "male" or "a man," leaving off the trans part entirely. That is fine if it works for them.

For me, it was a problem that I didn't recognize until it was pointed out by my therapist, who is very wise in these matters. I complained to her during one session that I felt "genderless," no longer a female but definitely not a male. She first questioned why that was disturbing to me, then suggested that I was, perhaps, not a male but a transsexual, a transman, different from the biological male with whom I was attempting to identify. She asked me to think about what it meant to me to be a transmale. And, because I am a good patient who subscribes to the notion that people can't be helped unless they are willing to help themselves, I thought about it.

I thought about it a lot. And I decided that she was right, which is why she's the therapist and I'm the patient. When I began to think of myself as a transman, something wholly apart from either a bio-male or a bio-female, a different animal entirely, I no longer felt genderless. I felt transgendered, which is what I am or which is, at least, an appropriate label to put on whatever this is that compels me to pay someone good money to stick a needle in my rear. I have accepted the fact that I will always be a transman, no matter how male I become, and, for me, that's okay. For someone else, it might not be. So be who you are and call yourself whatever makes you comfortable and happy. I call myself Matt. Oh, and by the way, did I mention that I'm a transman?

I have discovered, in speaking with hundreds of trans people in the last few years, that my early feeling of being "genderless" was not unique. Some actually embrace this feeling and attempt to maintain it. Others squirm, as I did, so completely socialized into our binary gender system that not connecting with a specific gender lends a feeling of rootlessness and instability. It was important for me to have a gender identification, even if it was a little left of center.

I thought that "transman" suited me well, but, although it appeared at the time that everything was finalized, that I had tied things up with a neat little pink and blue bow and decided to move on, secure in my label, the struggle was far from over. I flopped around more than a grounded fish, trying to figure out if I was a man, or just sort of a man, or only a man on Sundays or in months that begin with "J." I went out on a limb (a real short, skinny, teetery one) several times, insisting that a man was exactly what I was, only to revert eventually to the transsexual identity that I knew I would carry around, like those extra ten pounds that I gained from testosterone, for the rest of my life. But, when I went through my "manly" phases, I was not to be daunted by something as trifling as transsexuality. I was "passing," being seen as male by the outside world, which was a high so heady that it beat all the drug experimentation I did in college.

"Passing" plays an important role in the initial phases of transition. It is often how a transsexual person measures his or her progress on hormones. If I had a skill for invention, and if trans people had any money, I could probably live comfortably by creating a Pass-O-Meter that would track passing percentages and come up with a grand total of how "male" or "female" an individual was seen by the world. The problem with passing, however, is that the concept is built around the idea of deception—that a person is one way and is "passing" for something else. And, as I struggled through my "manly" stages, I wanted nothing to do with "passing."

WHY I QUIT PASSING

When I began this incredible journey, I measured my transition in terms of "passing"—how I was perceived by the outside world. My primary source of feedback was how often I was "sirred" as opposed to "ma'amed." If, on any given day, one out of four strangers called me "sir" instead of "ma'am," I assumed I was "passing" 25 percent of the time. As my metamorphosis continued, that percentage increased until, today, I could safely say that I "pass" 100 percent of the time. I *could* say it, but I don't. That's because I have quit "passing."

The concept of "passing" assumes that I am attempting to be something I'm not—that I am pulling a fast one on the rest of the world, getting by with some kind of false presentation. For myself, that is not the case. I am a man. I have no question about that and neither do any of the people I meet. That I am a man without a penis is simply an unfortunate fact of life, like being a man without an arm or a man without an eye or a man without a country. I don't "pass" as a man because I am one.

I believe that "passing" is a necessary concept in the first stages of a transition. It is a measurement of what is happening to you. Paying attention to it and talking about it psychologically reinforce what you are becoming physically. The milestone "firsts" are exciting and important—the first "sir," the first time you are directed to the men's room instead of the women's, the first time you flash your new driver's license at a club, the first time a gay man or a straight woman flirts with you. As you move through the stages, the "sirs" become commonplace and the once-in-a-while "ma'am" hits you in the face like a splash of ice water.

Then you come to a point when you start to realize that the "ma'am" never happens anymore—never ever. It hasn't happened for months. You walk into a group of men and you belong there. No one looks at you with a question in his eyes. The nurse at the ob/gyn clinic thinks you are some kind of pervert when you try to make an appointment. And the awareness sinks in—what you feel on the inside is what they see on the outside. You are a man. You are no longer "passing." You just are.

Some might argue that I am not a man because I don't have a penis. I prefer not to accept that rigid boundary. I once knew a man with cancer who had his genitals removed to save his life. I believe he was still a man. Those who would use the above argument would apparently say that he was not. I do not deny that I am trans and I come out as trans when necessary. I'm not ashamed of it. But I am a trans*man*. And I don't "pass" anymore. I just am.

Was I ashamed? Probably. This world doesn't cut trans people a lot of slack. But, philosophically, I was beginning to develop my current mindset about "passing," although I hold it now for different reasons. I don't profess to be a man now, except when forced to make a choice on some form that doesn't recognize alternative states of being, but I also don't see myself as "passing" just because the world sees me as male. I'm not tricking anyone. I'm just me. I have blended the female parts and the male parts of myself into a whole being. Granted, that being appears male, but that was my choice for the outside and is not necessarily reflective of what's going on underneath. Our society tends to put very finite expectations on male and female thought and behavior and has ways to punish those who don't conform. Although I continue to struggle with the rigid boundaries that the culture has put on someone who looks male, like I do, I have found freedom in incorporating the male and female pieces that were already there and not allowing myself to be bound by others' expectations of manhood. In other words, I don't have to wear a tie and I have a good excuse.

Part of the transition process is discovering how much blending of masculine and feminine is comfortable. Many trans people tend to go overboard at first, moving to the far reaches of masculinity (or femininity), becoming more macho (or femme) than someone who has always lived in the gender. This has a lot to do with insecurity and attempting to find a place on the masculine/feminine continuum. When the trans person starts to feel more comfortable with him or herself, he or she often gravitates back toward center, where male and female characteristics, as defined by our culture, can both comfortably inhabit one body. I was on a gender seesaw for a while, and, even today, I still have my "ups and downs."

WHAT MAKES A MAN?

I have been thinking about all the manly things I have done lately. There are far too many to list here, because anyone who knows me knows that I'm quite the macho guy, but here's a sample—crying for no reason while watching a particularly beautiful sunrise, making a woman kill a large, menacing spider, standing by while a woman with unusually strong arms hauled and tapped a keg, buying a bunch of color-coordinated flowers for my living room vase. "Okay," you're saying, "you must be kidding. These aren't healthy male activities." To which I reply in my nouveau-baritone, "Says who?"

Actually, they are completely manly behaviors, because I'm a man and I did them all. The difficulty in seeing these things as masculine behaviors lies in our culturally programmed internal definitions of what constitutes masculine and feminine actions, appearance and emotions.

We are socialized to believe that men do certain things and women do others. Men are expected to be brave, strong, aggressive, protective and to eschew emotion in favor of logic. And, unfortunately, many transmen buy into these externally imposed expectations and reject all things "feminine" before, during or after transition. We retrain ourselves to sit, walk, talk and act in specific ways that are deemed "masculine" by a society that is hell-bent on preventing any variance in the gender roles that were set up specifically for the purpose of maintaining our particular culture's status quo. We've been brainwashed, guys, and it's so internalized that we don't even realize we are being controlled by a force other than ourselves. As long as we allow society's definitions of maleness to control our actions and behaviors, we will never be "our own men."

So, all you manly men out there, it's time we listened to our own increasingly deep voices. We are the ones who can change gender as we know it in our world. We can be brave enough to let a woman kill a spider, we can be strong enough to admit that we don't know how to tap a keg, we can be aggressive enough to walk into that florist shop and buy flowers for ourselves and we can be protective enough to take care of ourselves, each other and the world so that we can long enjoy a beautiful sunrise. We can do whatever we damn well please, and act in any manner that defines us as people, whether that be playing tackle football, fixing a car engine, attending a musical at the theater or ironing our T-shirts and jeans (yes, I do).

My wise and wonderful therapist, who I have referred to here on occasion, says (and this is paraphrased, since I am not as wise and wonderful as she), "The kind of man you are is the kind of man you are." My late, great dad, in the true spirit of the Zen masters, used to say, "You couldn't have done things any other way because that's the way you did them." My translation of these quotable quotes is that, because I'm a man, anything I do is manly. If it doesn't fit with society's expectations, so much the better. Because when I can act how I act and do what I do and be who I am then I am truly "my own man," and maybe I can change the definitions of masculinity, at least in my own little corner of the world. Or get the crap beat out of me trying. And what's manlier than a black eye?

Although I struggled for an internal gender identity, going through phases of "real manhood" and "redefining manhood" and "incorporating the feminine into manhood" and "man, this is a lousy haircut, which is why I'm wearing this hood," society does not allow for any ambiguous selections when it comes to gender. However, the bureaucracy must think that we are not always sure ourselves, which is why gender questions on forms usually come with multiple choice answers. You can check "male" or you can check "female" but you never have the option of checking "all of the above" or "none of the above." I know several people, myself included, who created their own selection for the census—sort of a "write-in gender"—but I was told that, in those cases, the census takers just guessed, usually by looking at the first name on the form. In the United States, as in most countries, you are your papers. Whatever your driver's license, birth certificate and passport say determine whether you are called "sir" or "ma'am."

Each state has different laws and policies around gender reassignment and what makes a man a man (state governments are not, unfortunately, as ethereal as my therapist was). In my state, there are no papers or court hearings that will legally change a person's gender—the closest I could come was changing the gender on my driver's license. First I changed my name, then I changed my driver's license and now, no matter how insecure I'm feeling about my acquired masculinity (on some days, it changes by the hour), I only have to look at my license, see the "M," and know how I'm supposed to feel and behave. It's not so important to me anymore, but, early in my transition, I was treading water in the gray area between female and male, the area that made me, and anyone who came in contact with me, exceedingly uncomfortable. Hormones were taking hold, my hair was short and my clothes were masculine, but there was much about me that was still female. And on the planet where I live, knowing your own and someone else's gender is second in importance only to knowing which door leads to the men's room and which to the women's.

A TRANS-FRIENDLY WORLD? MAYBE SOMEWHERE OVER THE RAINBOW

I got my name changed the other day. I say it like it's no big deal, because it wasn't, really. At least not in Denver. It was easy. I went in, filled out five minutes of paperwork, plunked down my hard-earned $44, went in front of a judge and promised that I wasn't trying to escape my creditors (with all the money I owe, they'd find me anyway). I had written "gender reassignment" under "reason for name change" on my paperwork. The judge didn't question it. I walked out a few minutes later with an official order that stayed official as long as I published it for three consecutive weeks and sent proof to the court (in other locations, the procedure can be different).

Next stop, the Department of Motor Vehicles. The young woman who assisted me didn't bat an eye when I showed her the required letter from my doctor and my court papers. She just said, "Oh, we'll have to change that F to an M," did so, and then said, "Step over there, Matthew, and get your picture taken." At the Social Security office, the woman examined my papers carefully, punched something into the computer and said, "Okay, sir, your new card will be in the mail in about two weeks." Friendly, friendly people. Trans-friendly people. But it's easy to be trans-friendly when the proof is right in front of you. No matter how sensitive these employees were, they were still thinking, as most of us do, in terms of two genders. And they had legal paperwork to tell them which one of the two I was.

There have been other situations in which I haven't been so lucky. Nothing makes a trans person cringe quite as much as being "ma'amed" when he/she should have been "sirred" or vice-versa. After being "ma'amed" on several occasions when I thought I was passing fairly well, I have vowed that if I am ever in a service situation where I must greet an individual ("Can I help you, ma'am?" "Thank you, sir."), and I am unsure about the gender being presented, I will leave off the ma'am or sir entirely. There is truly no need for it, other than as a sign of respect, and true respect for a trans person is either correct gender acknowledgment or none at all. I propose that employees of every company be trained in these types of issues so as not to offend paying consumers of their products and services.

Another, even more important, aspect of trans life is the dreaded public restroom. I sweat more now that I'm on testosterone, but I never sweat so much as when I have to use the restroom at a mall or restaurant. A true trans-friendly business should have a unisex restroom in addition to the traditional men's and women's rooms meant for those stuffy people who define themselves by their genitalia. I would have appreciated this very much when I was passing but my driver's license still said "F." I would still appreciate it on those occasions when I'm not feeling so sure of myself and I can no longer legally use the women's room.

Even the "M" and "F" designations on driver's licenses can get in the way of identifying people as their true selves. There are people who prefer not to define themselves by gender at all. It must be difficult for them to have to choose an "M" or an "F" when an "N" or even an "N/A" category might be more appropriate.

Since I began identifying as transgendered, and later as transsexual, I have become acutely aware of how important

gender definitions are in our society. We truly do define
ourselves by our genitals, then cover them up, as if they were
our happy secrets. If we're going to identify ourselves by what's
inside our pants, then let's at least display it so everyone can
get a good look (and I can check out Ben Affleck). And, if
we're more civilized than that, let's take into account all the
gender variant people among us and make the world a more
comfortable place for them as well.

I have been accused of wanting to do away with gender
altogether. Those who have heard me speak or have read my
writing sometimes come away with the idea that I would
prefer one big blur of humanity, where people walked around
with male and female sex organs or no sex organs at all or any
combination of physical and psychological attributes that
would prevent any kind of gender designation. Actually, there
are plenty of people walking around right now who defy
specific gender designation—they may be transsexual or
intersexed or just plain rebellious—but they are out there
every day and they are doing society no harm. The harm is
done by those who insist that everyone must be in one of two
boxes, that "XY" equals "penis" equals "man" and "XX" equals
"vagina" equals "woman." These outdated equations
completely disregard anyone who is born with varied
chromosomes or varied sexual organs—primarily intersexed
individuals—and they also do not allow for transsexuals to
exist in any meaningful form at all.

I do not support eliminating gender designations—I only
support expanding them. Racial categories continue to
increase and far more adequately encompass the varied racial
and ethnic identities of our modern world than did the three
antiquated categories of my youth—Caucasoid, Negroid and
Mongoloid. I have not seen these used for years and no one
complains. Most young people have never even heard of these
terms. Racial identity is far more complicated than this and

we are far more evolved in our thinking about it, although we still have quite a ways to go. That some people identify with more than one racial designation is now commonplace. My fantasy is that, in the future, there will be several gender choices available, including the standard "male" and "female."

It is true that, simply by transitioning—injecting male hormones, undergoing chest reconstruction, taking a male name and wearing men's clothing and a male haircut—I have bought into a large part of society's binary gender system. When I am not being accused of trying to rid our culture of gender, I am lambasted for reinforcing narrow gender stereotypes. In fact, some transsexuals more rigidly conform to gender stereotypes than many non-trans people. For me, it is simply a matter of comfort with myself and with what I want to look like.

I admit that I am enamored with most things masculine. I like facial and body hair, low voices and a male body type. My physical appearance has a great deal to do with the identity that I have developed for myself, in stages, along the path of transition. That many trans people strictly adhere to gender stereotypes while others reject them has more to do with the identities that these people have forged for themselves before, during and after transition than with any need to make a political or social statement. Just like everyone else, who we are is reflected, at least in part, in how we present ourselves. Like snowflakes and those questionable chicken nuggets, no two trans people are alike. Each possesses a separate identity formed through an individual struggle with or against the tide, and, whether that identity is male, female, some of both or neither, it is definitely a part of the journey. Me, I'm a transman. Trying to be anything else is, at my age, just too darned exhausting.

CHAPTER THREE

TRANS BODIES

Hormones, glorious hormones. There's nothing like going through a second adolescence in middle age. Male puberty is a curious thing that is best undertaken by someone with a lot of youthful energy, exuberance and resilience—someone, say, thirteen or fourteen years old. But if you missed it the first time around, intramuscular injections of synthetic testosterone can recreate the experience so realistically that you can almost picture yourself in the middle school cafeteria preparing for a food fight.

TESTOSTERONE: THE PROMISE AND THE REALITY

I have the appetite of a 14-year-old boy and the metabolism of a 43-year-old man.

I have the libido of a 14-year-old boy and the dance card of a 43-year-old man.

I have the zest for life of a 14-year-old boy and the energy of a 43-year-old man.

I have the curiosity of a 14-year-old boy and the cynicism of a 43-year-old man.

I have the face of a 14-year-old boy and the body of a 43-year-old man.

I have the desire for junk food of a 14-year-old boy and the cholesterol level of a 43-year-old man.

I have the need for cool possessions of a 14-year-old boy and the credit card debt of a 43-year-old man.

I have the desire for freedom of a 14-year-old boy and the responsibilities of a 43-year-old man.

I have a 14-year-old boy's feeling that my whole life is ahead of me and a 43-year-old man's knowledge that more than half my life is behind me.

I have the dreams of a 14-year-old boy and the realities of a 43-year-old man.

And, boy, do I LOVE my life, man!

The first testosterone shot is probably the most eagerly awaited moment in a transman's life and one that is never forgotten. Although nothing much happens afterward, the recipient knows that he has crossed the threshold into a new beginning. There is a myth that the shot produces some kind of "high" or that the transman can literally feel the testosterone "kick in." In fact, the hormone sits in the muscle and slowly disseminates into the bloodstream over the course of several days. There are definite highs and lows as testosterone levels wax and wane in the system, but the hormone affects everyone differently. Some guys claim to become lethargic or feel "just not right" as the hormone dissipates and the time for another shot grows near. Others can forget their shot day (usually every two weeks) altogether unless they remember to mark their calendars. But it is not likely that a transman just beginning hormone therapy will lose track of the date for his next shot. Once the decision to transition is made, the changes can't happen fast enough.

I remember the day of my first shot—on Martin Luther King, Jr.'s birthday in 1998—when I sat in my therapist's waiting room, sacrificing my session to give her time to write the letter that doctors require in order to administer the hormones. With letter in hand, I telephoned my doctor's office with the news that I was officially qualified to begin hormone therapy. Undaunted by the fact that the receptionist was completely unmoved by this development in my life and tried to put me off until the next day, I pressed and pressed until she finally told me to come right over, since she was scheduled to get off work in two hours and probably figured she would have me on the phone until then if I didn't get my way. I arrived, breathless, at the doctor's office and left twenty minutes later with a healthy dose of testosterone in my butt and the fantasy that I would wake up the next morning looking like Rip Van Winkle. Unfortunately, it took several months for any hint of facial hair, but there was growth within a matter of days. When my friend told me that his clitoris grew almost immediately, I scoffed. But there I was, taking a shower four days later when I happened upon something quite unfamiliar.

"What *is* that?" I asked out loud in my then-still-soprano female voice. When I realized that the small, swollen protuberance under my fingers was not a fast-growing tumor, I was jubilant. I waited eagerly to see how much more it would grow. I'm still waiting.

But, like a young male on the brink of manhood, I was soon distracted by other concerns. Overnight, my sex drive rocketed through the roof. I think that, by now, it is sailing somewhere over Cleveland. I rapidly developed a new hobby and understood why unenlightened mothers warned their sons to keep their hands outside the covers. I also had a newfound understanding of the eighth grade boys who I used to teach. They were restless and inattentive and I often wondered if they had been fathered by space aliens. Now I knew, and, although I have no desire to return to teaching, if I did, I would be much more sympathetic.

Between the sexual fantasies, the activity that quelled them and running to the mirror every five minutes to see if hair had sprouted anywhere, there was little time for much else. I did manage to hold down a job, do some writing and engage in occasional social activities, but the excitement of a newly-hormoned body continued and I was certain that, any day, I would develop the manly appearance of which I had dreamed. Testosterone does miraculous things. It causes facial and body hair to grow, fat to redistribute, muscle mass to increase and vocal cords to lengthen, among other things. But I soon learned that it has its limitations—it can only act on what genetics have already programmed. Therefore, guys who disdain the hirsute can end up suffering hairy backs and shoulders, while guys like me, who covet body hair of any kind, can turn out disappointingly smooth. Guys who wish for a head of hair akin to Elvis Presley can wind up bald while those of us with thick, unruly mops long for some thinning. Just like our non-trans counterparts, we can only look to our relatives to determine what will happen to us. Since my own father was a hairless wonder everywhere but on top of his head, I believe now that my fate has been decided. No amount of male hormone will give me the wooly chest that I desire. But at least my chest is as close to a male one as the miracles (and expense) of surgery will allow.

Chest reconstruction is often the second major step in a female-to-male transition and it is a welcome subtraction to the household. One of the problems with transition, as in furnishing a home, is that you think you will be satisfied once you get that male haircut/get your name changed/get your driver's license changed/start hormones, but each progression only leaves you longing for more. The new couch would look so much better with matching end tables and the new body would look so much better without them. Chest, or "top," surgery is one of the most fulfilling accomplishments of transition. You can finally abandon painful and artery-constricting binders. You can wear the flimsiest of T-shirts with no telltale binder or bra lines. You can even take your shirt off in public. There are many doctors in North America and abroad who perform this surgery, with costs averaging anywhere from $3,500-$7,500 (save up, boy, insurance doesn't cover it). I chose a surgeon in San Francisco, one of my favorite cities, where I had high hopes of combining business and pleasure—but sightseeing with drainage tubes snaking loosely down both sides of my body proved less than ideal. Even so, the real attraction was the masculine chest that I would sport as soon as the bandages came off.

Breasts are a significant identifier of females in our culture and, therefore, something that transmen usually want to get rid of as soon as possible. When I was in my gray area of transition, when it was difficult to tell by looking at my face whether I was male or female, clerks, waitstaff and others who have a habit of calling people "sir" or "ma'am" were often stymied. I could see the confusion flicker briefly across their faces before panic set in and they jerked their eyes to my chest. If they saw any hint of a protrusion, which they did before my surgery, it satisfied them enough to address me as "ma'am." The "ma'ams" virtually disappeared after the surgery, even though my face was still the same for quite a while. Breasts are one of the strongest signifiers of gender, stronger even than genitalia, since they are visible to everyone, even through clothing. But it wasn't until after my surgery that I realized the insanity of our culture's insistence on sexualizing the female breast.

In the park, in broad daylight, with the same basic genitalia that I had possessed since the nurse wrote "Female" on my birth certificate, I could shed my shirt without any fear of being arrested or (unfortunately) ogled. A few short months prior, I could never have done such a thing. What was the difference?

REGARDING SEX, FAT TISSUE AND MILK DUCTS

I knew that female breasts were somehow a sexual thing long before mine actually were. At six years old, I donned my mother's half-slip, pulling it up under my armpits to cover something that wasn't there, then went next door to impress my best friend's brother, who was two years older than me. He was immune to my less-than-budding female charm and, like a normal eight year old boy, yanked the slip down to my waist. I burst into tears and ran home to report this violation to my mother, with Billy running after me yelling, "What's wrong? You don't have anything." Indeed, I did not, but I had a vague idea that even my childish chest should remain covered.

When I finally did "have something," I soon learned that it wasn't enough when the boys seemed to flock to my best friend, who, though less attractive, was more amply endowed. Although it would take a book to explain the adolescent and young adult psyche of this particular transman, suffice it to say that I always felt inadequate as a female—I never felt "female" enough—and somehow I came to the misguided conclusion that it was because my breasts were not big enough. For whatever Freudian childhood reason, I equated breast size with womanliness and I eventually decided that the only remedy was to get implants. So I did.

They helped for a while. I literally got at least twice the male attention that I had gotten pre-D-cup. It pleased me and it bothered me. Even as my boyfriends delighted in my chest, I questioned them as to their obsession. "Breasts are just fat tissue and milk ducts," I insisted, leaving out the silicone part of my own. "What is so great about that?" They couldn't answer me rationally. They were operating under the influence of testosterone, and I now, with more first-hand understanding, am able to forgive them this transgression.

I am coming to the point of my ramblings. I recently had reconstructive chest surgery. I now have a male chest, albeit one that looks like it got into a fight with Zorro and lost. And it has taken some time to come to terms with the fact that my chest is now asexual, at least in mainstream society. When my fellow FtMs asked to see it, shortly after the surgery, it took me a minute to realize that I wasn't going to be flashing them. Bio-male friends who I did not know intimately asked to touch it, then ran their hands across it with awe. I silently adjusted to the concept that they were not copping a feel. I still sleep in a T-shirt and boxer shorts and whenever I walk around my apartment shirtless, I worry about exposing myself to the neighbors. I could walk down the street now without a shirt and the only thing they could arrest me for is scaring little children. I could not be arrested for indecent exposure. My chest is not sexual anymore.

I truly love being able to wear a T-shirt now and not having to wear a bra or bind myself. By next summer, if my abs are good enough, I'm going to brave the world bare-chested for the first time. And, after 43 years of covering up, I'm going to feel naked. The weirdest thing will be that it's okay. This makes me question a society in which a few milk ducts and some fat tissue cause such lust in some and such shame in others that they must be hidden from view.

A female friend of mine says that she has always wanted to go to the beach or the park and be able to take off her shirt—not to show off, but for the comfort of it on a hot day. As long as we continue to sexualize the female chest, she will never have that option. I can only tell her what it's like. And that's unfortunate for all women who are sexualized by a part of their body that exists in order for infants to be fed.

I have recovered from feeling naked every time I take off my shirt. The surgical scars are still there and will always be with me (and quite visible, since my chest is still as smooth as Humphrey Bogart was in Casablanca). I have gotten used to them—I rarely notice them anymore, although I'm sure others do. The thing that keeps me shirted now, even on the hottest of days, is the lovely little beer gut that I developed when my body fat redistributed, an unfair consequence for someone who doesn't even imbibe. Men carry their body fat around their middles like inner tubes being hauled to a swimming hole. While I used to protest, as a female, that all those photographs of beautiful women in girlie magazines were obviously airbrushed, I say the same thing now about the models in men's fitness magazines. I'm sure that nobody really looks like that. The shirtless guys at the park playing volleyball? They must have their own private airbrushers following them around.

But when you have a transsexual body, you had better get used to being less than the perfect specimen that is touted in the popular media. Female-to-male headaches include being shorter than the average guy, having wider hips (we were originally made for childbirth and testosterone, as powerful as it is, does nothing to change the bone structure), sporting permanent chest scars and usually navigating a man's world without the one thing that society says all men must possess—no, not a fire-engine-red Corvette. Take another guess.

Penises are a very big deal (or a very little deal, depending on how you look at it) in the transmale community. Testosterone makes the clitoris grow, but usually only enough to be visible to the naked eye. Some guys have better luck than others, depending on genetics, but this is one thing you will never ask your father about, so you just have to wait and see. The question "Dad, how big is your dick?" is simply not uttered in polite families. But, once hormones take hold, you wish that you knew so you would have some idea of where you were (ahem) head-ed. The competition among transmen is fierce. Bragging about two inches, unheard of in the non-trans male society at "large" (sorry), is often standard fare at transman get-togethers. And those lucky enough to be able to afford phalloplastic surgery (the complete construction of a penis, which can run $60,000 and up in the U.S.) are definitely at the top of the food chain.

For those of us whose goals (and incomes) are more modest, there exists an array of prosthetics that can give the impression of a living organ inside tight jeans. I purchased the smallest size available for the unassuming bulge that promises only a little more than I can deliver. Since there was a buy-two-get-one-free sale, I took the seven-incher as an experiment, but it has since turned into a prop in my stand-up comedy routine. My stuffer has, on more than one occasion, flipped out of my briefs and onto the floor in the men's room, causing me to say to the terrified man in the next stall, "Uh oh. Better not sit down. You don't know what you could catch in here." I usually don't even bother to wear it now, so reminiscent is it of the tissue-stuffed bras of my youth. But with it or without it, the lack of a penis is always a visible reminder of my transsexual status. The real passport into man country is just beyond my reach. The longer I live as a transman, the less concerned I am about it, but the struggle has been ongoing.

Many transguys simply do not feel complete without the "real thing," a surgically constructed and attached penis. And, if finding a partner is a goal, the missing link becomes even more important. It seems to be a little easier for transmen who desire female partners—many women do not rank a penis at the top of their list of necessary attributes in a man. For transmen who are attracted to men, and thus considered "gay" because of their male appearance, it can be more difficult. And, as luck would have it (my luck, at least), I am one of those guys.

IS THAT A CHICLET IN YOUR POCKET OR ARE YOU JUST HAPPY TO SEE ME?

Stop me if you've heard this one—
Question: What do you call a gay man without a penis?
Answer: Single.
I was prepared for this reality before I even began my transition. Knowing my own fondness for this spirited male organ, and having some familiarity with the gay personals, I had an idea that sex and romance would not be forthcoming for a nouveau-gay transman. My gay male friends were discouraged

for me and some even questioned why I would make such a transition when I was getting plenty of sex as a female. That was an easy one to answer, since, unless you know something I don't, most of us spend more than 90 percent of our lives *not* having sex. That 90 percent should at least be enjoyed in the correct gender. They were still concerned that I wouldn't get laid, but neither did anyone offer himself up for the cause. No, I was on my own for this one.

Luckily, I had an acquaintance who was well versed in cruising for sex. He explained to me that I was lucky because I had small earlobes and small thumbs. Apparently, at least in his circles, men examined thumbs and earlobes to determine dick size. My luck, then, stemmed from the fact that if a man saw my hideously shrunken thumbs and earlobes and was still interested in me, he was not a size queen. It made me self-conscious, but it allowed me to blame my early rejections on the fact that I wore earmuffs and mittens to the bars in the middle of the summer. I considered surgery, but decided that, for the money I would spend, I could just hire one of those cute male escorts for twenty years. Celibacy even crossed my mind—that is, until my next testosterone shot.

But all that was early on in my transition, before I realized that there are worse things than being dickless in Denver. My genitalia has served me well for more years than I care to discuss, and will continue to do so—and did I mention multiple orgasms? It's not an idea to scoff at when you're mainlining male hormones in middle age. And, anyway, my own imagined inadequacy is probably nothing when compared to a male-born gay man who doesn't quite measure up. I wonder about those men who have teeny weenies, who are impotent, paralyzed, or in some other way don't possess the "let me worship your cock" accoutrements that seem to be standard fare for the community as portrayed in the gay media and in gay porn.

Since starting hormones several years ago, I understand the phrase "thinking with your little head." But what if it really is a little head? What if it doesn't function the way it should? If sex is only about a big, hard cock and seven inches is a little on the small side, what happens to everyone else? I have seen my share (and several other people's) of dicks in my lifetime and I know how much they vary in size, shape and capacity—it's not just a straight-guy thing.

Cock worship definitely has its place. I myself am intrigued by all things phallic—but I will never forget some of the little people who got me where I am today. Thumbs up to you, guys.

Trans sexuality can be as slippery as a newly waxed floor and I will slide into it in more detail later. Although I didn't transition to become a gay man, I knew that I would be perceived as such and that any potential partners would, at the very least, have to find male attributes attractive—but not all of them, only the ones that I possessed. My first rejection was the hardest (or should I say the most difficult). There was a blissfully ignorant period in the initial stages of my transition when I somehow believed that my lack of a penis wouldn't matter *that* much. I was a nice guy with an interesting life and a good sense of humor and people on the street didn't run screaming when they looked at me. How important could a penis be? I got my answer and it wasn't the one I wanted. But a broken heart is a small price to pay for being comfortable in my own body, even if that body doesn't "measure up" to everyone's standards.

DICKLESS IN DENVER
or
"YOU DON'T HAVE A WHAT?"

I try to write from personal experience, and, unfortunately, this is no exception. But it fits in with my spring has sprung (and I haven't) theme, so bear with me for the connection. I have recently been beating myself up over not having the proper equipment (you guys know exactly what I mean), even though it isn't my fault, it was the wily plan of that cruel practical jokester, Mother Nature. She's right up there with Father Time—talk about abusive parents.

Anyway, I experienced my first rejection (of many anticipated) due to my lack of appropriate appendages. What a blow to the male ego! I felt castrated (wait a minute, ohmigod, I am!). It was unpleasant, to say the least. But in the days that followed, after berating myself as a man and pummeling myself with the idea that I would never be adequate, I came to some realizations.

The first one is, I'll never be a bio-man. Now you're saying, "What is your I.Q.? You just realized that?" Actually, yes. I think that sometimes we get so caught up in the transition and the fantasies that we forget that there is only so much modern science can achieve. We wake up feeling male, go to bed (in my case, alone) feeling male and charge through our days feeling male. Then we look down and reality hits. And reality bites.

The second thing I realized is, maybe that's okay. For one thing, if I had been born male, would I realize what a gift that is? Would I appreciate it with anywhere near the intensity that I appreciate what I am now? Would I find joy in even the smallest changes in my body and in my world? Would I wake up each day like a little kid, eager to see what new discoveries, what new excitements, that day would bring?

And I know that, if I had been born male, I would never have had the unique opportunity to see the world from both sides, to experience both the female and the male aspects of life. That opportunity makes me the special person that I am and I don't know if I would want to give that up.

So as spring approaches and we once again see the beauty around us, as the sun warms us and hot young men take off their shirts (sorry), I think we need to take time to be thankful for the true gift that we have been given—the chance to love each day of our lives because we are better able to appreciate what we have, where we've been and who we are becoming.

I went through a lot of rationalization at first about not having a penis. It would have been nice to have something in my jeans that didn't drop out after I had dropped it in. It still would be. But I have learned to be comfortable with what I have (or don't have) and have managed to lead a fairly ordinary, yet fulfilling, life. As long as I keep my clothes on, I am a relatively unremarkable middle-aged guy. Underneath, I possess a trans body, which would be my legacy whether or not it had a surgically-attached penis.

Transsexuals have transsexual bodies, no matter how skilled our surgeons. And, in a society that values physical beauty and physical perfection, we are often left behind. As a female, I was bombarded with images of what I was supposed to look like and how much money I was supposed to spend to get that look. Most "fashion" magazines geared to women are primarily pages of advertisements, informing women, with glossy, colorful photographs and text, about what they must purchase in order to look like the women in the ads. Most men's magazines featuring photographs of women advise men on what they must buy if they ever hope to have women like that in their lives. The media, driven by advertising revenues, decides who we should be, creating an image that is just beyond our grasp but one that can surely be achieved if we drive the right car, wear the right clothes, choose the right makeup or buy the right magazine.

Although the body image hype of the consumer culture has been unusually hard on women, men are not immune, and they have been targeted with increasing frequency and with higher expectations every year. With the advent of the perfectly-bodied male, men's fitness and fashion magazines have flourished, more men are seeking cosmetic surgery and gyms and weight equipment are becoming as necessary for self-esteem as a solid bank account was in the past. With heightened emphasis on male beauty and male bodies, transman are put in an especially vulnerable position. Where do our bodies fit?

MEN'S BODIES, MEN'S BURDEN

Disclaimer: For once, this column is not about penises (well, mostly). I'm not even thinking about penises (well, not when I'm under anesthesia, at least). But this column is about body image, so I might mention penises, but only if they, uh, come up.

For years, women in our culture have labored under strictly prescribed body images (usually dictated by men and the fashion industry, which are often one and the same). Although the ideal female form changes based on what society needs from its women at any given time, it is still highly structured and generally unattainable by the majority. In recent years, eating disorders among women have increased dramatically and elementary school girls report that they are dieting. Our culture's expectations of its women can be unmerciful.

But what about the men? Men in our society have historically been immune to the destructive images presented as attractive. Of course, no one wants to have sand kicked in his face in front of his girlfriend, a la the Charles Atlas advertisements of my comic book youth. But, in general, men have been left alone to become soft, plump, bald and old without serious repercussions (especially if they have plenty of money). It is only recently that researchers have identified eating disorders in men, that men have begun to seek out cosmetic surgery and that an ideal body type has become specified for men and flaunted in the gay and straight media. The slender, muscular, well-defined and eternally young physique is now de rigueur for men. For today's studly guys, small butts, narrow hips, shapely pectorals and six-pack abs are almost more important than a six-figure annual income.

So where does this leave transmen? Yes, testosterone does

redistribute fat and put on muscle, but, face it, guys, we are never going to completely lose that butt and those hips. Hormones do not act on bone structure. And, although a few guys have told me that they have actually lost weight on T, it tends to pack on the pounds and bloat us like the Hindenburg. I haven't even mentioned the (here it comes) sexy bulge-in-pants that, for most of us, comes off at night along with our boxers. And I have yet to see an underwear model with surgical scar lines along his chest. We won't talk about receding hairlines.

Where this does leave transmen is either behind closed doors, covered by bulky sweaters in the middle of summer or totally redefining their sense of an acceptable male body. We can't look to the media to portray us or support us. We can't look to male-born men to model appropriate bodies for us. We can only look to ourselves and begin to construct our own male body image from the transsexual bodies that we have. Loren Cameron has done it. Billy Lane has done it. And so have countless other guys who have chosen many different body types to display proudly, whether they be muscular, large, thin, hairy, scarred, tattooed, pierced or whatever else fits an individual's image of his own male body. The problem with the media is that we are given only a well-lighted, airbrushed version of a human body. We never see the infinite variety of great bodies out there. But transguys know.

Penis. Oops, sorry, that just, um, "slipped out."

The transmen who I mentioned above are men who have been willing to create the bodies they desire and to display those bodies, clothed or unclothed, for all to see. Becoming comfortable with a trans body is a long and arduous process with a goal that many never achieve. As I have said before, to think of oneself as a man can sometimes make the process more difficult. To think of oneself as a transman, which might not be the ideal for many guys, at least allows for variations in the body that are not seen in media depictions of the male. Everyone's body is unique. The narrow images presented to us do not represent the majority of people who are born every day and live perfectly happy and normal lives. As transmen, we simply take our uniqueness a step further. My body works and I am lucky to have it. Do I want a penis, an unscarred chest, small hips and the perfect butt? I wouldn't turn it all down if it were offered, but it would also take away a part of me—that part that says I am unique.

The majority of people never see my naked body, where all the clues to my transness lie. This is good for me and, no doubt, a special relief for the majority of people. Once testosterone wormed its way into my cells for good, I began to look just like every other average Joe on the street (and, believe me, there are far more average Joes than there are guys who look like they just walked off a magazine page). Settling into a typical male role with others becomes commonplace after a time and I sometimes forget my transness until I look down in the shower. But, if you don't want to forget, just choose to transition on the job or in your neighborhood, around people who have known you for years. If you forget, they'll remind you.

AN OPEN LETTER TO MY FRIENDS WHO HAVE WATCHED ME TRANSITION

No, I have not grown taller. The ends of my bones fused in adolescence, which was thirty-some years ago.

No, my "sex change" is not what made me sick this year. I had pneumonia, then the flu, no doubt brought on by an immune system ravaged by too much job stress and too little sleep.

Yes, I remember when I used to wear high heels. The last time was over three years ago. If I decide that I want to go clomping in them down memory lane with you, I'll let you know.

Yes, I am aware that I have a moustache and a little goatee. I look at myself in the mirror every day when I get ready for work.

Unless you are preparing to sleep with me or have the letters M.D. after your name, please don't touch my hair, my face or my body if I haven't asked you to do so.

What is it about transition that gives folks the impression that they have free rein with your person and with your psyche? I have heard pregnant women complain that people, even strangers, walk up to them and touch their protruding abdomens as if they were small animals in a petting zoo. My friends walk up to me and run their fingers through my hair to comment on my haircut, point at or touch my face to comment on my facial hair and grab my arm to feel my muscle. They do this without asking, as if I am such an anomaly that manners aren't even necessary anymore.

One male coworker is constantly slapping me on the back, for no reason that I can discern other than in some misguided attempt to show me that he believes I am "one of the boys." I prefer not to be hit on the back unless I am choking, and, even then, I believe the Heimlich maneuver is the currently preferred remedy. Another coworker thinks nothing of walking up within inches of my face and examining it for facial hair.

Although I have been male in all areas of my life for three years, friends seem to take it upon themselves to constantly remind me of the "good old days," or to comment that my "sex change" might have something to do with my stress, any illness that I contract or the fact that my car keeps breaking down.

There is something to be said for relocating and starting over once you have transitioned. That something is, "Do it if you can." Unfortunately, I could not, and, since I could not, I would like to say to my non-trans friends,

"Back off." Give me a break, already. I'm not a monkey in a cage. I do not exist for your amusement or your fascination. I am a person with a right to privacy and space.

I do not say to you, "Remember when you were fat?" or "Oh, you seem to be losing your hair." I do not intimately examine your body that I have watched age over the past several years and point out the changes I have seen. I do not poke at your stomach and comment on your growing belly or get in your face to look for wrinkles. I do not believe, for any reason, that you are public property. I would only ask for the same courtesy from you.

(An open P.S. to all my non-trans friends: Thank you for your support over the years. I love all of you.)

Trans people are a curiosity to others, and there is no way out of it. Even those who did not know me before think nothing of asking me intimate questions when they find out that I'm trans, as if I'm not quite human after all. Those who did know me before, and know that I was human once, seem now to have their doubts. I write and talk about myself and about being trans, so I don't mind sharing pieces of myself with others, to educate them and, hopefully, to dispel some myths and prejudices. But being asked about my genitalia during a question-and-answer session in a human sexuality class is different from being asked about it over lunch in a local restaurant.

The problem I have is that it's difficult to encourage and discourage questioning at the same time. I believe that trans people will never be accepted and will never garner the same rights as non-trans people if we don't talk about ourselves, tell our stories and educate the world. When we are "out," we sacrifice some of our privacy and that is a choice we have to make. But chests, genitalia and visible physical changes are only half the story. Hormones also have a significant effect on our health and I rarely get asked about that. It's the boring part that no one wants to hear about. But it's important for transmen to take care of themselves, in ways that they never thought of before and in other ways that they would rather not deal with. Get healthy? Sorry. I have some eating, sleeping and smoking to do.

FTM HEALTH AND WELLNESS

While we are on the subject of our bodies, I would like to encourage all of you guys reading this to pay attention to your health. Along with the usual garbage about exercising, eating right and quitting smoking, I want to focus directly on the effects of testosterone and what transmen need to do to take care of themselves. Obviously, I am not a doctor, nor do I play one on television, so please discuss particulars with your physician and follow his or her advice.

Please remember that you need regular blood tests to monitor the following: cholesterol level, liver functioning, testosterone levels and red blood cell levels. You should also have an EKG on a regular basis. How often you are tested should be discussed with your doctor, with more frequent testing if there is a problem. T will often raise blood cholesterol substantially and it plays havoc with your good cholesterol levels (HDL). It is important to pay attention to this and adjust for it, such as cutting out high fat food and increasing aerobic exercise. T can increase the risks of developing cardiovascular disease, so pay attention. T is also processed through the liver, so liver function needs to be monitored. If you are on a weekly dose, pay special heed, because sometimes your liver can't metabolize the T fast enough and hasn't finished one dose before you shoot another. This can cause the liver to become inflamed, and, hey, you've only got one so you had better take care of it. Trans-plant has nothing to do with trans-man. If your T levels are too high, this can cause increases in liver problems and in red blood cell problems. Your doctor should be monitoring just where he or she wants you to be, level-wise. Increases in red blood cell count can put you at risk of stroke, as the blood thickens and the red blood cells tend to clump together. Testing for red blood cell count is not traditionally done, and many doctors do not have it in their battery of T-related testing for transmen. Ask for it. And don't forget to monitor your blood pressure.

Another area that is widely (and understandably) ignored by guys is pelvic exams and pap tests. If you still have your organs, you can still have problems with them, even though they are not working. In fact, because they are not working, you might not notice certain concerns. Pre-transition, if you were bleeding excessively or painfully, you would go to the doctor, as this could be a sign of problems. Without your period, you might not have this symptom. Also, uterine, ovarian and cervical cancers are just as deadly now as they were before you transitioned. Yes, it's embarrassing to make an appointment with an ob/gyn in a baritone voice. Yes, it's embarrassing to sit in the waiting room in a full beard. I pretend I'm waiting for my wife until I'm called in. The last time I went, the nurse called me up to the desk and asked, in a waiting room full of women, why I was there. In my best casual voice, I said, "Pap test and pelvic exam." She said, "Oh," and I sat back down, almost smugly. Leave 'em wondering, I always say.

Oh, and watch that weight. T can put on the pounds and it also distributes the fat, as most of you know, in a male pattern, that is, around the midsection. This fat pattern has been linked to heart disease, so close the refrigerator and open the door—go for a walk or run, take off that weight and let the muscles show through (easy for me to say, a lot tougher for me to do).

I won't say anything about quitting smoking, at least as long as I still smoke, but the primary thing to remember is, no matter what the hassle, expense and sometimes embarrassment of regular medical attention, think of the hassle, expense and sometimes embarrassment you went through to get where you are. You have finally made it. Now is the time to start your life, not end it. Don't cut it short. Live the life you were meant to live and make sure it's long and healthy.

Taking care of our bodies and maintaining our health are often more difficult goals than they should be. There is a great deal of prejudice in the medical establishment with regard to trans people. That reassignment surgeries and most hormone treatments are not covered by insurance is only a small part of the problem. Routine, and even emergency, medical care is sometimes impossible to get and the attitudes of medical professionals toward trans patients have cost some their lives. Tyra Hunter, a male-to-female transsexual, died after a car accident when emergency medical technicians discovered her penis and discontinued treatment at the scene, choosing instead to laugh and make jokes while onlookers pleaded with them to help her. Robert Eads, a female-to-male transsexual, died of ovarian cancer after over twenty doctors refused to see him, saying that they did not want to deal with him or that they did not want him sitting in their waiting rooms. These are documented cases of medical neglect resulting in death.

Another male-to-female transsexual was left to lie in her own vomit for twenty minutes in a hospital bathroom because the doctor found her so repugnant that he did not want to enter the room. I was told by an angry doctor in my HMO that I was going to die if I didn't stop taking my hormones, even though there was nothing in the minor problems I was experiencing to indicate that. I didn't stop taking them and, to paraphrase Mark Twain, reports of my impending death were obviously greatly exaggerated. But I could tell from her apparent rage that she did not find me appealing and was having a difficult time working with me. In fact, I have noticed a distinct change in how I have been treated by my HMO since I transitioned. In all fairness, however, I have not been denied care. But there are many others who have, as evidenced by the examples above, and this is only the short list.

Medical professionals should know better. They have taken an oath to provide the best possible treatment for all. There should not be categories of people who are not eligible for appropriate medical care. One of the biggest fears that transsexual people have is of getting sick and having to be hospitalized. To be at the mercy of an uncaring, and sometimes hateful, health care system is terrifying. There is no excuse for what happened to Tyra Hunter and Robert Eads, and there is no excuse for continuing neglect at the hands of medical professionals who are entrusted to save lives, not take them.

As trans people, we take our bodies to a level that we are comfortable with in our transition, then we take care of them as best we can and go off and live our lives. Those lives are usually pretty insignificant if you use the universe and infinity as standards of measurement, but they are ours nonetheless and we have a right to them. In the last half-decade of my life, I seem to have offended a great many people just by existing. I have been told that I have no right to do what I did and that I have no right to change my body as I have. It's amazing how indignant people can become when someone who they have never seen before and will never see again does something that has no effect on their lives whatsoever. The people closest to me have been able to accept my changed body. They have been able to deal with my experience and what they have experienced in the process. Their feelings, and what I think about myself, are really what is most important. It's my (trans)body, after all.

CHAPTER FOUR

TRANS SEXUALITY

No, I don't mean transsexuality, which is the business of being transsexual. I mean trans sexuality, which is the business of being sexual. Being transsexual doesn't have a whole lot to do with the act of sex, although I'm sure that there are some trans people out there who are getting a whole lot luckier than I am. The "sex" part of "transsexual" refers to biological sex—the maleness or femaleness of someone. "Trans" means to go across or to change. Therefore, transsexual means to go across or change sexes, and has no relationship to physical intimacy or attraction.

I am frequently asked "Who do transsexual people have sex with?" Presumably, this is a legitimate question, since we are assumed to be an alternate species and therefore incapable of completing the sex act with anyone who is not from Alpha Centauri. The answer, of course, is that transsexual people have sex with their partners, their one-night-stands or whoever they have chosen to have sex with. Transsexual people have sex organs, regardless of what surgeries they have or haven't had. We still have orgasms (another question I have been asked). We are as creative with our sexuality and our sexual activities as anyone else. And our gender identification has nothing whatsoever to do with our sexual orientation.

Gender identity is the term used to describe how a person feels about him or herself—what gender that person feels he or she is. Sexual orientation is the term used to describe who that person is attracted to—what sex/gender/hair color/eye color/body build/personality that person is physically and emotionally drawn to. Once that distinction is made, another confusion follows rapidly on its heels—"If sexual orientation doesn't change, how could you be straight as a woman and gay as a man? You changed your sexual orientation." In fact, I did not—my label just changed.

People are sexually oriented to men, to women, to both, to some combination of the above or to no one. Yes, this does leave out those people who will only date someone from Alpha Centauri, but they are few and far between. "Gay," "lesbian," "straight" and "bisexual" are labels, not orientations. And the interesting thing is that these labels are applied based not on the gender a person is attracted to but based on the gender of the person feeling the attraction. As a female, I was considered "straight." As a male, I am considered "gay." My sexual orientation, which is to men, hasn't changed. My label has changed because my own gender has changed. My label has nothing to do with who I am attracted to. It has everything to do with who I am.

GAY LIKE ME

When I announced my decision to transition to male after living forty-two years of my life as a straight female, my friends reacted with shock and dismay. Their first concern was what I would do with my wardrobe, complete with several pairs of four-inch spiked heels. Their second was who would get what (and that was just the guys). After they finished fighting over my Donna Karan blazers, they actually began thinking about the finer points of gender reassignment—like who I would sleep with.

"So you like women now?" one of my female friends asked,

eyeing me warily as she prepared to move if the testosterone should happen to kick in at that moment.

"No," I said. "Why should I?"

She seemed relieved but still suspicious. "Well, you're straight, aren't you?"

She was not the only one who mistook a label for a sexual orientation. Several others asked me if I was going to start dating women, since, of course, everyone knew I was straight. Therein lies the question that our species has been grappling with since the dawn of time—if a straight female undergoes gender reassignment, what, then, is his sexual orientation when he comes out on the other side?

I can't speak for the multitudes, but I can tell you that my sexual orientation is, and always has been, to men. Whether that makes me gay, straight, or something else entirely is a question best left to those whose job it is to come up with labels. Gay, lesbian and straight are labels assigned to sexual orientations based on the sex and gender of the person feeling an attraction. They have nothing to do with the sex and gender that person is attracted to. As a female attracted to men, I was straight. As a male lusting after the same guys, I'm gay.

This amazing concept helps explain my ability to easily change sexual orientations, a feat that has yet to be accomplished by anyone in Exodus International. I didn't change orientations, only labels. However, I soon discovered that calling myself a gay man didn't go over well with one particular population—gay men.

As a public speaker, I have presented to gay and lesbian groups over the last three years and have offended some gay men in the audience who claim that (a) I'm not a man and (b) I'm not gay. The men who got angry with me when I mentioned that the "gay community" tended to be phallically oriented were the first to insist that I could not call myself a man because I didn't have a penis. They went on to tell me that I was not gay because I did not have the "gay experience" in my life.

I will grant them that I do not have a penis (actually, I have several, but I usually keep them in my underwear drawer). I will also concede that I did not have the "gay experience" when I was growing up, even though that experience is probably quite different for someone growing up in the heart of San Francisco and someone growing up in the heart of rural Nebraska. The only problem I have is with the cumbersome language that it takes to actually describe myself—a transsexual man who is attracted to men. "Gay man" is so much easier to say. But, to avoid upsetting those who are aware that I am phallically challenged, I have adopted a moniker that satisfies me—gay transman. That's my label and I'm stickin' to it.

Suddenly being gay, or at least being considered as such, has been an interesting adjustment. So has loosening my grip on the straight mainstream's idea of sexuality. I have often considered how much easier it would be if sexual orientation could be changed, if the label constituted the loving and I could be as "straight" in my new body as I was in my old one. Holding hands with a woman while walking down the street, putting my arm around her at the movies, giving her a kiss at the mall—all would put me right back into the comfortable, acceptable world from which I came. And it might be easier for me to find a partner. Many straight and lesbian-identified women have no problem dating a transman. There are even some women who seek out transmen as partners. They are attracted to the male physical attributes and are equally drawn to the fact that the transman has experienced aspects of femaledom that a non-trans male will never know. This boyfriend knows how to treat a woman, has a healthy respect for her and knows what she wants, sexually and otherwise, because he's been there. Whether or not he has a penis does not seem to be a major issue. But, as logical as this arrangement might appear, especially for a transman like me, sexual orientation remains unchangeable and I retain my newly bestowed label.

BECOMING GAY

I lived the first forty-two years of my life as a heterosexual. I have lived the last three years as a gay man. Far from being in denial about my true orientation, I have, in fact, lived it voraciously from the time that I developed my sexuality in adolescence. I have always been attracted to men—I just haven't always been one.

The notion, so prevalent in the gay and straight communities, that transsexuals undergo gender reassignment to deny their homosexuality, makes as much sense as the idea that a lung cancer patient has a lung removed to deny the fact that he needs to breathe. In reality, he would undergo this painful and frightening operation in order to keep breathing, to keep living, just as transsexuals want to keep living in bodies that will allow them to do so. Expensive, complicated surgeries and sometimes dangerous hormone administration are not undertaken by someone just to make his or her sexual attractions more acceptable. Anyone who would submit to such a project has an unshakeable identification with the gender opposite of the one assigned at birth.

I was never a lesbian. However, I tried valiantly. At puberty, when I first began to experience gender confusion, I did everything in my power to explain it away by attempting to convince myself that I didn't really want to be a boy, that I really just liked girls. I wrote in my diary about the cute girls at school. I left secret love notes in their lockers. I traded my prized purple pen to my best friend for a five-minute make-out session. The most discouraging thing about these endeavors was that I felt nothing. I felt nothing for the cute girls receiving my love notes, nothing for my friend. After a year of doing everything possible to become a model lesbian, I had to admit to myself that it was all a failure. I wasn't attracted to girls. I was attracted to boys. But yet, I wanted to be one. It made no sense to me and, in 1967, there were no resources for a twelve-year-old to learn about gender identity issues. So I buried my feelings and went on to live my life as the straight woman that I was, at least on the outside.

The only positive thing that came out of my junior high experience is that I am living, breathing proof that sexual orientation cannot be changed, no matter how desperately that change is desired. I would have given my right breast to be a lesbian (instead, I gave up both of them). It would have explained everything. It was not to be, though, as my attraction to men took me through two marriages and several relationships while the little voice in my head kept saying, "See, you can't be a man. You're attracted to men." It took another thirty years before I realized that sexual orientation and gender identity have nothing to do with each other. Gender identity is who you feel you are. Sexual orientation is who you are attracted to. If these concepts were related, there would be no gay men or lesbians (or there would be no straight people, depending on how you want to look at it).

Once I understood that the fact that I felt like a man and the fact that I found men irresistible were mutually exclusive, I was able to explore my gender identity and make some decisions about what I would do. Since undergoing gender correction, I have entered the gay community. As a transman, my sexuality is far more complicated than labels will allow, but because I identify as male and am seen as a man by society, I am labeled gay. I don't have a problem with my sexual orientation. I know what it is and I live it every day. My life as a transman and as a gay man is full and satisfying. The fact that I am sometimes more acceptable to those in the mainstream straight community than I am to those in the gay and lesbian community is my only confusion.

In recent years, some transsexual people, regardless of sexual orientation, have aligned with the gay and lesbian community and have requested (or demanded) inclusion in that "movement." This has not been well-received by some gay men and lesbians, who are not keen on the addition of a "T" at the end of "GLB." In fact, it does belong there. For all of us, it's about gender—not the gender we like, but the gender we are. Unfortunately, it has been a hard sell. The gay and lesbian community has often rejected transfolk in the larger scheme of things. Their primary arguments, that our communities have nothing in common and that strange and crazy trans people will destroy the credibility of the mainstream GLB movement, are positions that I am all too happy to dispute.

UNI"T"ED WE STAND

Although the Y2K panic proved to be little more than an excuse to party like it's 1999, initials are still in the forefront of controversy as we move into the new millenium. The "GLB community," if there is such a solidified entity, continues to be divided over the idea of adding the dreaded "T" to the end of its name. A recent survey in *The Advocate* revealed that an equal number of readers favored and opposed this addition. The National Gay and Lesbian Task Force (NGLTF) includes transgender in its mission statement. The Human Rights Campaign (HRC) does not *(note: they did not at the time I wrote this column)*. And each individual has his or her own opinion, including transsexual people who identify as straight men and women and have no desire for inclusion in what they see as a marginalized group—the GLB community.

The two primary reasons given by those gay, lesbian and bisexual people who would exclude the trans population from "their" movement and from their quest for equal rights are that trans people have nothing in common with GLB people and that trans people are so "weird" or "sick" that they will bring down the rest of the movement. Maybe you have used these arguments yourself. If you've got a minute and an open mind, I've got a rebuttal.

First, to quote Riki Wilchins, Executive Director of GenderPac, "gender rights are human rights," regardless of whom the HRC considers human. While I may not agree with Wilchins on everything, I am in agreement with this point. Gender variance has as much to do with the GLB *and* the straight population as it does with transfolk. Research has shown that the majority of people who exhibit "gender variant" behaviors in childhood (i.e. "feminine" boys and "masculine" girls) grow up to identify as gay or lesbian, not as trans. As these children get older, they are singled out, harassed and physically assaulted based on their behaviors and gender presentation, not on their sexual orientation, which is usually unknown unless it is announced in some way. A survey by NGLTF, in conjunction with GenderPac, found that 28 percent of adult GLB respondents had been discriminated against due, at least in part, to their "gender expression."

Straight children, teens and adults who are harassed and attacked because they are perceived as gay or lesbian usually exhibit some type of gender variant behavior or appearance that results in such a perception. It is not the orientation that invites such abuse. It is the gender presentation or gender variant behavior. Gender identity, which can be shortened to "T" just to keep the initials rolling easily off the tongue, is, without a doubt, a GLB issue.

The second argument, that trans people are "weird" or "sick," is the same argument used by the religious right against GLB individuals. For all you GLB folks reading this, in 1972 you were as nuts as I am. You're okay now only because homosexuality was removed from the *DSM* (the manual professionals use to diagnose mental illness) in 1973. If a person with a penis in a dress is weird and sick, I wonder about all the drag shows I see when I go to the gay bars (I won't even talk about Halloween). And what's up with the new drag king shows that are attended primarily by lesbians? It seems that transgendered presentations are acceptable to a point, as long as they wash off at the end of the night.

TRANIFESTO 71

Of course, not all GLB people exhibit gender variant behaviors or appearances. Nor do all trans people. I know some extremely masculine men and some very feminine women who have corrected the gender mistake of their birth and who identify as straight, mainstream men and women. They would no sooner desire to be included in the GLB movement than would Newt Gingrich. That would be far too "weird" and "sick" for them. But even they don't have the right to marry who they choose, can get fired from their jobs or dismissed from the military and risk getting beat up or even killed because of who they are. We have the same issues.

Pride 2000 is approaching. Let's work together, folks, so we can love who we want, dress how we want, act how we feel most comfortable and be who we are. And thank you to the many GLB individuals and organizations who support T inclusion in the movement and equal rights for everyone. United we stand—GLBT.

Gay men, lesbians, bisexual people, transfolk—we all have something in common. The core of our commonality is gender—we are labeled and discriminated against based on our gender. The second layer is the form that discrimination takes—murders, assaults, destruction of property, failure to get jobs or housing, inadequate health care, the inability to marry, the denial of partner benefits and society's narrow definition of "family" that does not include us. And while I am busy trying to convince some gay men and lesbians of this, I am equally engaged in trying to convince some transfolk of the same thing. Yes, transphobia runs rampant in the gay and lesbian community, but there is no lack of homophobia in the trans community as well. While some gay men and lesbians are scared off by any association with transfolk, some, maybe the majority, of trans people feel the same way. They identify as straight, have assimilated into the larger mainstream community and want no association with the "fringe" element that they consider the gay and lesbian population to be. They buy into both arguments that the GLB community has established—we have nothing in common and, that by aligning with the GLB community, our own quest for equal rights will not succeed.

HOMOPHOBIA IN THE STRANGEST PLACES

"I don't want to look like a faggot."

"Is there no getting away from you people?"

"I'm not going to a gay bar. I'm not a fag."

These are actual comments to which I have been subjected—by transmen. Homophobia is not relegated to the straight non-trans population. It is alive and well in our own community, a community that ought to know better. I have had transmen gape in disbelief when they find out I am gay.

"I've never heard of a gay transman," they will comment.

I have heard others say that they want nothing to do with the gay and lesbian community.

"Those people are just too weird," they say.

Oh, please. Like being a transman is as mainstream as shopping malls and cell phones. Coming out as gay in the trans community can be as difficult as coming out as trans in the non-trans community. There are transmen who feel that any alliance with the gay and lesbian community is wrong and can only lead to trouble. They have transitioned into straight, middle-class lives with wives and children. They want no identification with a population who they see as "different" or "deviant." Never mind that they suffer the same discriminations as gay men and lesbians. Never mind that, in most states, the straight marriages they cherish are really considered same-sex marriages and could be invalidated in a heartbeat if their birth sex was discovered. Never mind that, when they die, their wills can be contested and their wives left with nothing. Never mind that there are transmen who have been left to die because they could not get appropriate medical treatment, especially for non-male illnesses. Never mind that they could be denied housing, loans or jobs if their birth sex came to light.

Medical treatment, property rights, marriage, jobs, housing—these are the issues of gay and lesbian politics. These are issues that assimilated transmen feel are their birthright. Forgive me, guys, but speaking of birthright, what did your original birth certificate say?

Homophobia in the trans community is not just an inconvenience for trans people who are subjected to homophobic remarks. It is dangerous and deadly. It prevents us from joining with the one community who, when they are not wallowing in their own transphobia, might help make a difference with legislation that will benefit us. It prevents us from joining in our own community as a solidified political block. It keeps us divided. It causes us to reject potential allies—and each other.

With so much animosity going on between various factions in various communities, wouldn't it just be easier if trans people kept to themselves and joined with their "own kind?" It might be, but in many cases, the only thing trans people have in common is the fact that they are trans. Trans people come from so many backgrounds and have so many varied interests, hobbies and political, religious and social affiliations that, like anyone else, they tend to gravitate toward groups and individuals who share their beliefs, opinions and lifestyle choices. A fifty-year-old Republican transwoman would probably have little in common with a twenty-year-old Democratic transman and people can only discuss their surgeries for so long before they start to nod off.

I have often been asked if I would consider having a relationship with another transman, as if our similar genitalia would make us the perfect pair. Early in my transition, I refused to even entertain the idea. I wanted a man with a penis—not just any old penis, but a fully functioning, natural one. Being less than perfect myself did not seem to affect my choosiness in any way. At the time, I had only met a few transmen, most of who were just beginning their own transitions and so showed little of the masculine traits that I found attractive. I simply could not picture myself with someone so much like me. Part of this, certainly, was my insecurity about my own masculinity, but I held firm (or maybe not so firm) in my belief that a biological penis attached to a masculine, male-born man was the only way to go— until I attended my first major female-to-male conference.

CATHARSIS

Oh, those life-changing events. As if transitioning wasn't enough, I recently had what I consider to be a cathartic event in my newly male life. I attended a conference—my first female-to-male conference ever, *Forward Motion,* in Los Angeles last October (*note: October, 1999*). Just seeing about four hundred of us in one place was exciting enough and would have been well worth the price of admission. But what happened to me was so much more than that.

If you are a regular reader of this column, you are used to me moaning about my anatomy (no, not those extra few pounds, those are muscle). I'm talking about what I don't have. Well, lucky you, you're not going to hear that anymore. Because I went to Los Angeles with two assumptions about myself and left three days later without them (I think they're floating around somewhere over the ocean, trapped in the LA smog). Those assumptions were: that I need to have a dick to be a man and that a man needs to have a dick to be *my* man.

Both assumptions died an instant death within the first twenty-four hours when I saw, sat with and interacted with hundreds of men who were penisless. There was no doubt in my mind that these were men. There would have been no doubt in anyone's mind. In fact, anyone who might have accidentally stumbled upon that conference could have easily assumed that this was some men's retreat weekend, which, in fact, it was, with some supportive women and female presenters sprinkled into the mix (and so as not to insult anyone, I need to point out that some guys identify as other, neutrois or androgynous). I'm sure that some of these guys had dicks, but due to the sorry state and the expense of current phalloplasty, my guess is that most did not.

These were men, folks, and not only were they 100 percent male, there were so many who were 100 percent hot stuff that I pretty much forgot my phallophantasies for the weekend. There were way too many other nasty little things going on in my brain.

All in all, it was a fantastic weekend, an excellent conference with interesting workshops and a chance to play, shirtless, in the ocean. I left California lighter on baggage, but with more friends, a couple of crushes and a whole new way of looking at things, including an even more fluid definition of male, female and gender itself. Although I have a great deal of respect for those who identify as completely gender neutral, I still like masculinity and still define myself as male. But now I have an even broader notion of what a man is and what it means to be male, thanks to all the great guys I spent time with that weekend.

That conference really was one of the defining moments in my struggling, middle-aged male adolescence. I will never forget the gorgeous men I saw there and how this helped with not only my own self-definition, but with my notion of what and who I was attracted to. The most interesting thing about the idea of dating another transman is that others would see us as two gay men in a relationship. Those pesky labels are impossible to escape. Of course, that wouldn't bother me. But it might bother the one guy who I picked out of the crowd, the one who I couldn't stop thinking about long after the conference was over—the one who I discovered dated only women. No matter. The most important thing for me was losing my phallo phascination. But the impact of his existence continued to linger long after I found out that he was unattainable. Isn't that always the way it goes?

TRANS ATTRACTION— IT COULD HAPPEN

For forty-two years, I was a straight female, extremely attracted to every aspect of maledom (with the exception of beer guts, hairy backs and the idea that farting is hilarious). I was especially fascinated by the nifty parlor tricks displayed by a particular male organ (no, I don't mean the intestine—see above). This jack-of-all-trades, so to speak, allowed for standing elimination, sexual interaction and was, in the case of some of my former lovers, the perfect bite-sized after-dinner treat. It could go from alpha sleep to a twenty-one gun salute in a matter of seconds. It provided hours of entertainment—far better than solitaire, although it could, and often did, play that game in my absence. It even re-created itself in gizmos such as remote controls and bright red sports cars, no doubt designed by natal men. And it was never sexier than when it was perky and ready for action, outlined in a tight pair of jeans. When I transitioned, I knew I could settle for nothing less—not on me, what do you think I am, a millionaire? No, on my lover. I knew that my lover would have to possess a functional penis.

Not only was this a non-negotiable requirement, but, because I have plenty of room to be choosy (this is a joke, folks), I also knew that any future lover would have to have lived his entire life as a male. I have nothing against females, mind you. Some of my best friends used to be females. Some still are. It was simply the idea of maleness, male energy, male bodies and male psyches that triggered responses in the reptilian part of my brain. I knew who I was and I knew what I wanted. And, because I had that idea permanently imbedded in my very being, of course I got the hots for a transman.

What's the big deal, you ask? Everyone knows that transmen are hot stuff. Right? You had better be saying yes. But the point is, I didn't know this until that magic moment, across a crowded room and all that sappy stuff, when I swear that even my soft silicone pants stuffer was standing at attention. At that instant, I knew that I wanted to sleep with this guy and I couldn't care less what he had in his pants or what sex was written on his original birth certificate.

Nothing happened and nothing ever will. That doesn't matter. What was important about the discovery was that it not only changed the way I viewed other transmen, it changed the way I viewed myself. I feel that this event, which was, unfortunately, completely internal, was nothing short of cathartic for me. It opened up a whole other world of potential partners. It opened my mind to the idea of "queer sex," not necessarily defined by the boundaries of man-woman, woman-woman or man-man. It made me realize that a relationship between two people, sexual or otherwise, has little to do with genitalia or bodies. I finally understood that the brain truly is the biggest and most erotic sexual organ. And I also understood that people (men, women or other) who insist on a penis being naturally attached to their partners are definitely missing a whole dimension of sexual and romantic experience.

I am still attracted to maleness. However, my definition of maleness and what I find attractive was forever altered by this experience. For that, my fellow traveler in this gender journey, who shall remain anonymous, I thank you.

To date (or not to date), I have not been with a trans person romantically or sexually. I have a lot of trans friends and I am very active in the transgender "movement," which is happening in our country and in the world, no matter who we join with politically or otherwise. And, although I still call myself "gay," it is primarily for the benefit of people who feel the need for a one-word definition of my sexuality— people like, well, me.

CHAPTER FIVE

TRANS PRIDE

It might sound strange to take pride in something that has nothing to do with winning the Nobel Prize, saving a life or discovering a cure for cancer, but cultivating self-pride is an important step for people who have been shunned, ridiculed and, basically, treated just downright nasty for a long time. I have been called "very sick" and "very brave" and I don't believe I am either. I am just a person struggling to get by in the world, like everyone else, while dealing with life's little practical jokes. In my case, one of my issues, along with the fact that there is never enough money, that I'm getting older every day and that mechanical things always break down, is that I am a transsexual. It never goes away, just like impending death and yearly taxes. It's not a curse and I am not a victim. It's just a fact.

Although trans people have a diagnosable mental illness in the eyes of the psychiatric community, my belief is that the basis for any emotional stress suffered by transgendered people is society's strict definitions of gender and the refusal to accept anyone who is "different." It's a "chicken or egg" dilemma that the medical and psychiatric communities are still trying to figure out—is transgenderism in itself a mental illness or does any mental illness a trans person might exhibit come from society's expectations of and limitations on gender? Is there a physical component, some synapse in the brain that's firing differently or a prenatal dose of the wrong hormone? Or do people choose to be transgendered (for the fun of taking hormones throughout life, having multiple surgeries and being rejected by society, I guess)? At this time, no one knows. Maybe we will never find out and, if we don't, does it matter? It is simply the way some people are, whatever the reason, and, by taking pride in ourselves, we can take back the power that has been siphoned away from us, pick ourselves up, dust ourselves off and move on. Let's get over it, already. The choice is ours.

A MATTER OF CHOICE

Think about these three questions:

Did you choose to be transgendered?

If you could go back to your conception and change it, would you?

If you knew before your own child's birth that he or she would be transgendered and you could change it, would you?

Got your answers? Here are mine: no, no and no.

Here's another question:

If you have made a gender transition, did you choose to do so?

Got your answer? Here's mine: yes.

All these questions reflect the concept of choice. As trans people, we often relinquish our own ideas of choice and free will, allowing ourselves to become the victims of our births. We like to say, "I didn't choose to be transgendered. I was born that way. It's not my fault. You should feel sorry for me, not hate me." Although it's true that none of us chooses to be trans, here are the unspoken messages we are sending when we say these things:

"I didn't choose to be transgendered *and if I had the choice, I would choose not to be.* I was born that *horrible* way. It's not my fault *that I'm a freak.* You should feel sorry for me, not hate me, *because I'm a poor, pathetic victim.*"

How much better it would sound, how much stronger we would feel, how much prouder we would be and how much more power we would have if we said instead:

"I didn't choose to be transgendered *but I would choose it if I could.* I was born that *wonderful, fascinating* way. It's not my fault *that I lead such an interesting, unusual life.* You should *not* feel sorry for me, and not hate me, *because I'm not a victim or a freak, and I have a lot to teach you.*"

I didn't choose to be transgendered, but I did choose what I was going to do about it. People don't like to hear that. Non-trans people don't like to hear it. It makes them angry because, for some reason, they seem to think that they should have control over what I do with my own body. Trans people don't like to hear it because they are afraid that, if any part of being trans looks like a choice, we will not be able to receive insurance coverage for medical and therapeutic assistance. Newsflash: we don't get it now. And, regardless of what benefits *should* be allowed to me because I'm trans, I refuse to let anyone take away from me the idea that I have personal power, personal freedom, control of my own body and the right to choose who I am and what I do.

When we deny that anything we are or do is a choice, we are giving up a great deal of personal power. We create a victim mentality that turns us into children at the hands of the larger society and the medical and psychiatric establishments. I don't need other people to decide when and if I should transition (they did, but that's another article). I don't need to live my life around other people's time frames, decisions and the misguided theory that they know what's best for me. I am not a victim of my transness any more than I am a victim of my brown eyes or my small feet. I control my life and I control what I do with it. As long as we refuse to acknowledge personal power (and personal responsibility) in our decisions, i.e. choice, we give up huge parts of ourselves to the control of others.

And what if a "cure" is found? What if scientists discover a "trans gene" or an "abnormal" brain region? If a cause for transgenderism is found, can a cure be far behind? We may eventually be able to determine, in the womb, whether or not a child is transgendered. What will this mean for us? It could mean that we will someday be able to "fix" a transgendered child even before he or she is born. Or, if we can't, we can just get rid of that poor, pathetic freak before he or she has to suffer the consequences of a transgendered life. The ramifications of this are too terrifying to think about.

I don't want to be "cured." I'm glad I'm alive. I love who I am. It's not me who needs to change but society, our culture, our way of thinking about trans, gay, lesbian and bisexual people. But as long as we allow ourselves to be victims, as long as we deny ourselves the power of our own choices, as long as we leave the unspoken words hanging in the air, we encourage our own infantilism by others and we encourage the cause and cure mentality that could do away with "our kind" forever. No, thanks. I'd rather have a V-8. Or a shot of T. Think I'll go do that now, since it's still my choice.

The idea of having a choice is right up there with the uppity position of being proud of who we are—it makes people angry. But we all make choices every day. And choice equals personal power equals pride. As trans people, we should not give up the power to make our own decisions to the extent that we can. Unfortunately, there is a world out there that would take that power from us, sometimes in the guise of doing what is best for us, as if we are not intelligent adults and cannot possibly act in our own best interests. If we don't speak up, if we don't make ourselves visible and let our voices be heard, if we don't come out and let people know who we are, our lives, and our destinies, will continue to be decided for us. We will continue to be discriminated against, receive substandard medical care, lose our jobs and our housing and even our lives. For transmen, who so easily assimilate into the mainstream male community due to the strength of testosterone, the temptation to disappear can be overwhelming. To be "out" is to risk everything. But that will never change if we make ourselves scarce. Come out, young man. And be proud of who you are.

When I first began my transition, I fancied myself a man and saw my future as one of adaptation to and assimilation of traditional male roles and identity. However, my resolve to quietly enter manhood and remain there lasted about as long as my first dose of testosterone. I come from rather politically rebellious roots—my parents staged a sit-in long before there was a name for such a thing, in the early 1950's, in order to integrate a Nebraska hotel. They spoke their minds, championed the civil rights of all people and let their liberal politics be known. Although they are both long dead, I knew that they would not sit back and let the civil liberties of any group be trampled on without speaking out and attempting to educate others. I knew that, no matter how comfortable it was in the closet, it would be a tight fit, and I tend to be claustrophobic. And I also knew that transsexual people would never be recognized, would never be given the basic human rights that others take for granted and would never be understood unless some of us were willing to speak out, to be heard and to teach others about us. I accepted the challenge and now write and speak about transsexual issues to groups, classes and corporations—and that's where the pride comes in. It's difficult to get up in front of a group of people and talk about anything, especially yourself, without a measure of pride in who you are and what you stand for. I found this pride early on in my transition and it has never left me.

TRANS PRIDE

On St. Patrick's day, everyone is Irish. And on Gay Pride Day, everyone is . . . well, I guess that's where the analogy breaks down. I remember my first Gay Pride parade, which I stumbled upon quite by accident, my intention for the morning being to lie in the sun at Cheesman Park and get a tan. As I spread my towel on the grass, it was hard not to notice that people were gathering in a large and festive group and they certainly weren't there to look at my pasty white legs. I asked a woman what was happening. "It's Gay Pride Day," she announced, with a look that said, "What cave have you been living in and why don't you go back?" As a person not only in professional denial of my transgenderism but of any sexual orientation issues that status might bring up, I stayed and watched the parade, just for the fun of it. And it was fun.

I had never seen so many happy, no, downright joyous, people in my life. I had never seen so many colorful costumes, so many decorative floats and so much diversity, from leather and motorcycles to ball gowns and high heels. I was hooked. I went home two hours later, humming "If My Friends Could See Me Now," and wondering a little at my overblown fascination with it all. It would be seven years and seven Pride parades later that I would finally come to terms with my own gender and sexuality issues. Once I did, I came out with a vengeance. But, hey, I had good role models—entire parades of them, people so proud of who they were and the larger picture they stood for that they were marching down the streets of Denver announcing themselves to anyone who cared to look.

For trans people, pride is just as important, although sometimes more elusive. Our numbers are smaller, our position in society more precarious as laws passed to include even gay people don't include us. And, like our gay brothers and sisters, in most places we can still lose our jobs, our apartments and our basic civil rights just for being ourselves. We are hated sometimes, we are feared sometimes and we are made fun of. But we exist, and we still have that right. We are brave and we can be proud of that. And whether you shout it from the rooftops or think it to yourself in your own little corner of the universe, you know who you are, so be proud of it. This year, I'll be marching in the parade for the first time. Look for me. I'll be the guy who looks really proud of himself.

I did march that year, and every year after that, waving one of the three homemade signs that I had concocted—"Support Your Local Transman," "Testosterone: Breakfast of Champions," and "Transmen Tie One On." For a period of time, I had great fun just being a transsexual. The transition was exciting, I was going through a male puberty in middle age and I no longer had to restrict myself to socially sanctioned gender roles and expectations.

Many transmen, regardless of age, go through a period of adolescent thought and behavior brought on by body changes and the unfamiliar and overpowering sensations of testosterone. It levels out eventually and the frightening thrill of change, the rabid sexual desires and the adolescent silliness dissolve into real life. You still have to make a living and pay bills. You still have to interact with people in the world. You still have responsibilities, the expectations of others and the day-to-day requirements of whatever life you have established for yourself. Regardless of how you feel inside or what you know to be true, the world sees you and responds to you as a man and you have to figure out how to do "male" correctly or, at least, acceptably, if you want to remain safe and maintain some semblance of the life you have already built.

But the remarkable thing about a gender transition is that you can add on to the foundation of your previous life or you can tear down the whole thing and start over from scratch. You can keep as much of yourself as you want and fling the rest of it into the wind. You can be—or you can become.

METAMORPHOSIS

My dad had a saying for every life event. None of them was original. He picked them up along the path of his life and pocketed them like a stealthy shoplifter, then brought them out at opportune times as if they were his own. I remember all of them and each one has some meaning for me. The one that's floating around in my head and in my life right now is "Do what you've always done and you'll get what you've always gotten."

I bring this up now because spring is upon us, when a young man's fancy turns to love and this old man's fancy turns to things unprintable, but, nevertheless, spring signals new life and rebirth to all of nature. And, more than any other life form, we as trans people are allowed the opportunity to be reborn. We can literally start new lives at twenty, thirty, forty or seventy. We alone get a second chance to live as we have always wanted and to be the person we have always dreamed of being.

Most people wallow through their lives relying on past experiences, some good, some bad, to shape their current reality. They want to change, to break away, but they can't. They are locked into the definition of self that they have created. They say, "I can't do that (stop eating, play basketball, learn to fly an airplane, whatever) because it's just not like me." Or they say, "I've always been that way. I can't change now. That's just me." And they keep repeating the same damaging patterns or refuse to try something new because they are locked into an image of who and what they are that doesn't include change.

Trans people are change personified. We can, and do, reinvent ourselves, physically and otherwise. And the best thing about reinvention is that we don't have to be stuck in the self we were before. We can create entirely new beings out of the ashes of our former selves. Just because Terrence did things one way, there is no reason that Teresa has to. Paula may have felt one way about something and Paul may feel entirely differently. We have the power to create from scratch the person who we most want to be.

So when you're watching the flowers bloom and grass spring up and the trees start to bud, remember that you don't have to do what you've always done. You can do whatever you want to do. And you can get far more than you've ever gotten. It's all in you—whoever the heck you are.

So, as we go about changing, weeding through our lives to discard what no longer has meaning and add what is most important, it's imperative that we remember how we came to this place and to take some measure of pride in what we have accomplished for our lives. To paraphrase my former therapist: "Our surgical scars are the visible reminders of our battles as trans people." Wear them well.

But with pride in ourselves and the optimistic view that we can, eventually, change the climate of our culture, comes responsibility for others. We cannot expect non-prejudicial treatment if we are not willing to give it ourselves. It starts within our community. We must reach out to trans people who, for whatever reason, might not have access to the information and services available—those on fixed incomes, seniors, the differently abled and those in rural communities. We must be inclusive of minorities and attempt to overcome language and cultural barriers in our outreach. We need to tear down some of the hierarchical structures that we have erected in our own community that say that those who are "fully transitioned" are somehow better than those who have decided against surgical intervention, or that those on hormones are somehow more "legitimate" than those who are not.

Then we must go outside of our own community to join with and support our allies and to fight discrimination wherever we find it. There is no room for homophobia, racism, ageism, classism or any other kind of prejudice in our own movement or outside of it. We need to be visible in our support of civil rights for everyone, trans and non-trans alike, and become allies for other groups and movements. Hatred destroys. As we request others to keep an open mind about who we are, we must open our own minds and resist the urge to keep such a tight focus on our own issues that we fail to see what is going on around us.

TRANS-CENDING DIFFERENCES

About ten days after the World Trade Center attacks, I received an e-mail from a Middle Eastern country. No, surprisingly, it was not from their top-level government officials asking for my advice on how to proceed. It was, in fact, from a transgendered female asking for advice on how to get help with a gender transition. In his/her country, such things are nearly impossible.

Unfortunately, in my country, such things are nearly impossible as well, and I could be of little help to this person, other than to refer him/her to a resource in the Middle East. But the exchange was interesting for several reasons.

First, amid everything that is happening in my country and in his/her own, the daily rigors of individual life, including dealing with gender issues, continue. The need for mind and body gender congruity is so strong that it outweighs other concerns, like personal safety, and other questions, like "Am I going to be alive tomorrow?"

Second, it demonstrates that everyday citizens of the United States are trusted by everyday citizens of the Middle East and, no doubt, elsewhere as well. This individual took a big risk in writing to an American. With what has taken place here and abroad, including mass anti-American demonstrations by many in the Middle East, his/her letter could easily have been rejected or worse. Of course, it wasn't, and perhaps this person recognized that, under all the political trappings of both our countries, we are all human beings at the core.

And, finally, this letter proves that, regardless of race, ethnicity, religion, nationality or any of the dozen other markers that we use to divide us, we have similar issues, similar wants, desires and dreams.

I wish I could have helped this person. I have not heard from him/her again and I hope that all is well. I also hope that we in the United States can realize that our similarities to people everywhere are greater than our differences and that we need to work hard to recognize our fellow human beings when we see them—no matter what they are wearing, where they are worshipping or where they live.

There has been a lot of hatred floating around since September 11. Arab-Americans and Muslims are reporting hate crimes and discrimination directed at them in many cities in the United States. Many are living in constant fear in a country that is home to them. Almost all Americans are living in fear as well, but Arab-Americans have been singled out for attack by citizens of their own country—other Americans.

As trans people, we know what it is like to be the targets of prejudice, discrimination and hatred. We know what it is like to see people in our own community murdered because of who they are or what they look like. We know the fear of leaving our own homes, walking on the streets, shopping or going to an event because of what might ensue if we are recognized as trans. I ask that we not let our emotions get the best of us at this time. I ask that we not administer to others the hatred and prejudice that has been inflicted on us. I ask that we do not fear what is different or what we don't understand as others fear us. We must not let these trying times divide us because, as we can see from the letter I received, we are all pretty much the same.

Every individual is responsible for working through his or her own prejudices and, hopefully, becoming a better person for it. As a community, we as trans people must not tolerate bigotry of any kind. If we have the power to change our bodies, we have the power to change our minds. Let's make sure that we are not participating in any behaviors toward others that have been used against us. It is the only way that we will all succeed as the strong, proud people that we are.

CHAPTER SIX

POST TRANS

For some transsexual people, there truly is a post trans—
a period that begins when they believe they are integrated
enough into their new gender to be a complete "man" or
"woman" and ends when they die. They assimilate into their
new gender, possibly marry and adopt children and leave
any trappings of their trans past behind. For me, there is no
post trans. I will always be a transsexual. But there is definitely
a post transition, and it is the space in which I now live,
where I am satisfied with the hormonal and surgical changes
that have occurred, where I don't have to introduce myself as
a transsexual to everyone I meet and where I don't have to
pretend that I'm not one, either.

I have struggled through the initial stages of transition. I
have managed to moderate the overwhelming sex drive that
began with my first testosterone shot. I have cultivated enough
facial hair to please me and, although my body is not as hairy
as I would like, I have come to accept that smoothness is the
genetic legacy left to me by my male forebears. I have gotten
to the point where shaving is a hassle, not something to look
forward to. I have figured out an acceptable male wardrobe
after much trial and error and a lot of expense for clothes I

didn't like but thought I should have as a man. Although some of my friends love to don a suit and tie as a visible presentation of their maleness, I can't tolerate the constriction and use my transness to justify wearing a T-shirt or an open collar underneath a blazer for dress. If I'm going to be a nonconformist, why not go all the way? Although my chest will always be scarred, I have come to accept it as a part of me. My pants stuffer is most often found in my drawer instead of my drawers. I no longer turn, or even feel the urge to, when people say, "Ma'am. Oh, ma'am." I know they aren't talking to me. I have become invisible, just another guy on the street. Maybe I have male privilege—I don't know what it is or how to identify it if I do. I'm just living my life in the best way that I know how and trying to educate and entertain some people along the way. If I've done that, then it's been worth it.

JUST ANSWER THE QUESTION, PLEASE

I have recently embarked on a major project (why, after going through gender transition, do other projects still seem major?). I'm putting together a collection of my columns and some other ramblings that will be available later this year through the miracle of self-publishing (you don't really think that major publishing houses are fighting over who gets this little gem, do you?). Anyway, in order to do this, I have had to go back and sort through everything that I have written in the past four-plus years. It's kind of like looking at your naked baby pictures—some are really cute and some make you cringe. But what I noticed most about my array of columns are the inconsistencies in my thought processes and opinions (unlike my baby pictures, where the only inconsistency seems to be that they are photographs of a baby girl).

I see my columns carrying me through some real identity crises and a lot of struggling with the concepts of maleness and manhood. I seem to go back and forth between defining myself as a man, a transman, a transsexual and a Martian (not really, but I needed another word to make the sentence flow). Considering myself fairly well-adjusted, I can only draw the conclusion that this gender thing is a lot more confusing than I would like to believe and a lot more unusual than I generally think it is.

I was recently asked the question "How do you see yourself as a man in this world?" Even after all the soul searching, as evidenced in my columns, I still don't have a good answer for that. The answer I came up with, just to have a response, is that I don't see myself as a man in this world. I have no realistic idea of what it's like to be a man in this world. I also have no realistic idea of what it's like to be a woman, but I have a much better notion, having lived in that guise for so many years. But I think that, as transsexuals, we have misplaced so many large chunks of ourselves, or they have been misplaced for us, that it is difficult to answer certain questions. We have been "cheated," in a way, in the socialization that we didn't get, in peer group encounters that didn't happen for us and in life experience that grants other people membership in the "man" and "woman" clubs and sometimes leaves us on the outside with our noses pressed to the window.

I don't know the secret password to get in. I haven't decided yet if I even care. But I do know that I'm far too old and far too busy with other things to spend a lot of time worrying about it. And I sometimes feel that I'm far too old and far too tired to come up with acceptable answers to the other mind-boggling questions that I get asked when I do presentations on being trans, such as:

What made you feel like you should be a man? *I don't know.*
How do you feel different now? *I don't know.*
Do you feel like a man now? *I don't know.*

Are you happier now? *I don't know.*

How can you justify changing your gender just because you didn't feel right? *I don't have to justify it.*

Do you think you're better off now? *I don't know.*

Lame, elusive answers to legitimate questions from people really seeking to understand what they perceive as an alternate universe and what I usually perceive as a normal state of existence. After almost a half-decade of writing about this and thinking about this and living this, I still can't come up with any good, satisfying responses. But at least they're consistent.

When the band stops playing and the lights come up, you still have to go home with yourself. And, since you and yourself are keeping steady company, you damn well better like who you're spending all your time with. If you can't accept the part of you (or the whole of you) that is trans, you will pass a lot of time being miserable. Having to constantly cover up what you say or do out of fear of discovery can be a long and tiring endeavor.

But being a "professional transsexual" can be exhausting as well. There are times when I just want to walk away at the end of the day and hang up my transness like a McDonald's employee hangs up his uniform. Even a conversation about the weather would be a welcome relief. If I don't come out to you right away, or ever, it's not because I'm ashamed of myself or who I am. It's not because I want to trick you, betray you or keep a secret from you. It's because I want to talk to you about literature or art or music or politics or movies or even what you want for dinner. I want to hear about who you are and I want you to see who I am, underneath the trans body and all that goes with it. With that in mind, when I do come out to you, ask away—and then let's talk about the weather.

Even though I have, so far, decided not to adopt a post-trans identity that includes ceasing to identify as a transsexual and slipping quietly into the mainstream of society, there are still many adjustments I have had to make because of my appearance. Society expects different things from its males than it does from its females, and getting used to that has probably been the most difficult part of the whole journey. In the beginning, I trained myself to do things that were foreign to me, such as open doors for women and stand when I am introduced to someone. I learned how to give a firm handshake while making eye contact and get drinks for female companions at parties. These things come naturally to me now, but there was a clumsy education process that most guys go through at puberty or before, with at least one male role model to help. Some non-trans people are surprised that these things don't come naturally to transsexual people, but, as I said earlier, socialization is a powerful persuader and I was definitely socialized as a female. But becoming a self-taught male in middle age has been an interesting, and enlightening, experience.

Public restrooms offer one of the most frightening challenges known in transville. New transmen have a variety of worries, including what message they will send by sitting down in a stall rather than standing, man-like, or using the urinal and how their urine will sound as it hits the water. I had those fears as well and used to float unused toilet paper in the bowl to muffle the sound of liquid smacking into liquid. I have since learned that nobody cares, or even notices, which way my feet point in the stall and that everyone's urine sounds about the same no matter what vessel it is coming from. It has been a while since my stomach has tightened at the thought of using a public men's room, but it is definitely one of the steepest cliffs to scale.

Once the toilet trauma was behind me, I had to learn to navigate through the obstacle course of maledom, while non-trans men called me "Buddy" and treated me as if I had always been a member of their secret society. I was subjected to crude comments about the female anatomy when a man sitting beside me at an outdoor concert assumed that I would appreciate (or appreciate degrading) halter-topped women as much as he did. I discovered the impact of Chinese food on my auto mechanic's intestinal system in a conversation that he never would have had with me when I was female. And I learned that if I accidentally pulled in front of someone in traffic, I would get flipped off, cursed at and generally have my life threatened.

I have also gained some very useful information. When I was female and my tire went flat, I would stand by the car until someone stopped to help. Two years ago, when I got my first flat as a male, I got out and waited patiently—for about sixty seconds—before I realized that no one was going to pull over. Thirty minutes later, I had not only actually read the owner's manual for my car but I had successfully changed my own tire. This led to instant popularity at work, where I am now expected to change tires for others as well and to carry heavy objects (lift with your legs, not your back), move furniture and reach things in high places, even though I have not grown a millimeter.

Gay male interaction has its own lessons. It took me several minutes to realize that the man who was displaying himself to me on a darkened street was not a flasher. In the park, when I nodded at a man who was sitting on a bench, I meant the gesture as "Hello." He understood it as "Let's go," and headed for the nearest clump of trees, turning to see if I was following him. When I realized what I had set in motion, I disappeared faster than day-old donuts at my office. At the time, I was not yet acquainted with the subtleties of gay courtship. I now know that, although a kiss may still be a kiss, a nod is not always "just a nod."

One of the most curious, and disturbing, developments of being male in the world has been the almost palpable fear of some women who encounter a man on the street, especially after dark. There are women who clutch their purses tightly when they pass me, as if I am going to snatch them. Some women, at night, will cross the street, as if I am going to snatch *them*. This might be flattering, knowing that I am so fully perceived as male, if it weren't so confusing, offensive and, well, sad. I hate the fact that *some* men have done *some* things to *some* women that are reflected in the fear and uncertainty of these behaviors. I hate that women don't feel safe to walk on the street and I hate that *any* woman does not feel safe around me. Having been where they are, I understand the apprehension. And, being where I am now, I understand that it must be stopped and that men have the power to stop it—in many ways.

HANGING 'EM OUT TO DRY

If you live in Colorado, you might be aware of the recent brouhaha (I've always wanted to use that word) about the Boulder Public Library and the American flag. It seems that the library sponsored an art exhibit by Boulder Safehouse, a battered women's shelter, entitled "Art Triumphs Over Domestic Violence." Included in the exhibit was a piece that featured ceramic penises (I've always wanted to use that word) of various colors strung up on a clothesline. The piece was called "Hanging 'Em Out to Dry."

These colorful penises apparently hung without comment in the library for several weeks, but a problem arose when an employee asked about hanging a giant American flag over the library's outer door. When the manager refused, saying that it might alienate some people and pointing out that American flags were displayed elsewhere in the building, a controversy ensued. That controversy came to a head (I've always wanted to use that word) when a "thief" somehow removed the penises in protest. The dangling organs were later recovered unharmed and the self-proclaimed dildo bandit turned himself in. He said that he was only trying to make a statement about the importance of hanging the flag as opposed to stringing up a bunch of phalluses in a place that is often frequented by children.

Much fuss was made of the unpatriotic head librarian, the suddenly-obscene artwork and the innocent little minds that could forever be traumatized by such a blatant display of disembodied male organs. Editorials were written and radio talk shows had a heyday. Two camps were formed—those who were shocked that a dick display that had gone unnoticed for weeks was allowed to hang in the library when the flag was not and those who believed that the rod wrangler was violating Safehouse's freedom of speech by removing the dismembered members.

Unfortunately, no one seemed to address the real problem, which, in my opinion, had nothing to do with the American flag and everything to do with why penises, and, by association, their owners, are seen as symbols of violence that need to be "hung out to dry." I am not saying the artwork was wrong. What I am saying is that we need some dialogue here—men and women talking about why the artist and other women who supported the artwork feel that men need to be strung up.

Believe me, I am well aware of the pain, fear, physical injury and even loss of life that battered women suffer. I have been a social worker for almost two decades. What concerns me is that art is symbolic and the ceramic penises are obviously a symbol for men in general. Some of the men who I have heard discussing this issue are outraged that the library rejected the American flag but hung the penises.

And they should be outraged, but not for that reason. Their outrage should come from the fact that some of their brothers have caused some women such misery that those women feel it necessary to symbolically dismember or hang men. They should be outraged that someone has hurt these women so much that they express themselves with art that is undeniably anti-male. They should be outraged enough to open up a dialogue with women, to show women that men can be trusted, that they are not cruel and vicious and hurtful and that penises are not the problem. And they should be outraged enough to tell their battering brothers that enough is enough and then do something about it.

We are (rightfully) appalled at the way members of the Taliban have treated their women. Our politicians have self-righteously spouted about the abuses that the Afghan women have suffered in recent years. We say that we want to change it, to give these women back their rights and their dignity. We should be equally appalled that the women of our own country feel the need to display hanging phalluses as a symbol of their anger and fear. Patriotism is not at issue here. The hate, hurt, anger and disenfranchisement of battered women are the issues. Wake up, men of America—oh, and check your underwear.

There are a lot of excuses that violent men can give for their behavior toward women—the aggressive nature of testosterone (sorry, guys, I'm on it, too—that one doesn't fly), their socialization, the (almost) unlimited power men are given in our culture and the fear and anger that arise whenever that power is threatened—but none of these are valid. I said earlier that we are not "opposite" genders. I know that now, having lived as both female and male and having interacted with the world in both genders. We are more alike than different and we need to stop living on different planets and start living on earth, together.

Trans people can and should be at the forefront of any gender "movement." We should share our experiences and the insight that we have gained from living in two genders (regardless of how we perceive ourselves and our gender identification, transsexuals have faced the world in two genders). Those of us who embody both genders, who have taken the masculine and feminine parts of ourselves and put them together, can be especially helpful in teaching others, both trans and non-trans, to accept, integrate and cherish both the masculine and the feminine in people and in the universe. There is something about the blending of the two genders that takes on an almost spiritual quality and certainly causes appreciation of the world from two different points of view. With this knowledge and this experience, we can work toward healing divisions between men and women—divisions that have no purpose and no need to exist—and end the curse that has been inflicted by the establishment of "opposite" genders. But we can do this only if we first acknowledge who we are.

There are many transsexual people who eliminate their pasts. This is, in my opinion, an outdated recommendation that some very traditional therapists and support organizations still champion. These people are told to get rid of all photographs, change all documents and destroy any evidence that indicates that, prior to transition, they existed at all. I take issue with advising any person, but especially someone middle-aged or better, to deny over half a life. Regardless of the quality of that life, it had an affect on the person who lived it. It molded and shaped that person in many ways. Ridding oneself of one's past might allow a person to move into the post-trans, assimilated identity to which so many aspire, but to deny a former existence is to deny a large part of oneself. It might work for some, but it would never work for me.

WHY I WON'T CHANGE MY BIRTH CERTIFICATE

Okay, maybe if I meet a rich, handsome fellow who is living for the day that he can whisk me off to Europe for a romantic vacation and I have to get a passport, I might consider changing my birth certificate. But only if I can't get a passport without doing so. Otherwise, the record of my existence on earth will stay as is, for a couple of reasons. And what are those reasons, you are wondering? Glad you asked, because if you weren't curious, you would stop reading right now and I don't write this thing just to kill time.

The number one reason why I have decided not to change my birth certificate to reflect my current name and gender is because, for me, the person who exists now is not the person who was born in the Midwest on March 17, 19 . . . , um, well, sometime in the mid-1900s. That person was a female with a different name. And that person is reflected on that birth certificate. The way I feel about that person and that life, at least at this point, is not so negative that I want to destroy any record that she ever existed. For the same reason, I have not destroyed pictures of her or mementos that prove that she lived. Instead, I have incorporated the parts of that identity that I liked or am pleased with into the new identity that is me. For me, to change my birth certificate and to destroy pictures and keepsakes is a denial that a large part of my life ever existed. It is like throwing away forty, um, forty-some years of my life and saying that they never happened. I was born a female and denying it doesn't change it. This is not the right path for everyone, and I respect the need for someone to choose a different way.

The second reason that I choose not to change my birth certificate has more to do with my political beliefs than my identity. I have been married twice in my life as a female, and, to be honest, I really don't ever want to be married again. However, if I meet someone and fall in love, the activist in me says that hauling my birth certificate down to the marriage license bureau in full beard and baritone and legally applying for a license to marry a person with a penis would be the ultimate political statement. Standing on the courthouse steps with my man, he with his man, being legally married by the Justice of the Peace—well, can't you just see it, girls? But don't expect me to wear a wedding dress. My birth certificate may say "Female" but my driver's license has a big ol' "M."

Even without the political motivations, I have still not been moved to change the record of my birth. I firmly believe that a female baby was born that day. That life did not disappear the day that I decided to transition. And I believe that, whether I change my birth certificate or not, unless I have a penis, my death certificate will probably say "Female." Most coroners, it seems, are not too hip when it comes to the whole transsexual thing. The only record of my life on earth as a male or a transmale will be in my writing. But I don't remember being born and I'm not going to remember dying, so the thing that really matters is what I did with the life I was given in-between those two events. I'm still working on it.

FREQUENTLY ASKED QUESTIONS: HELPFUL INFORMATION FOR NON-TRANS PEOPLE

As a very "out" transman, I do a lot of public speaking, primarily to non-trans audiences. What follows are selected questions that I repeatedly get at my speaking engagements. I hope they are of help to my non-trans readers.

What does your family say and how do they feel about your transition? What about your friends?

My parents have been dead for some time. I have only a sister who had a difficult time at first and has, over the years, softened her opinions and has attempted to accept me as I am. There is a rather large age difference and we have never been alike in our interests and pursuits, but, regardless, she has lost a big sister. I have always chosen my friends based, in part, on their open-mindedness and acceptance of the diversity in the world around them. I lost no friends in the process, although I know that other trans people have. Some trans people have very open and accepting loved ones. Others have become permanently estranged from, or disowned by, their families because of their gender transitions. Often, loved ones will eventually (and gradually) have changes of heart and reaccept the trans person into their lives.

One of the things that trans people often fail to realize and fail to deal with is that a transition, for those on the outside looking in, is like a death. A loved one is dying and friends and family members are helpless to do anything but stand by and watch. People in transition are often very self-absorbed without meaning to be. They are undergoing changes that they have waited a lifetime to experience and they sometimes forget that their excitement is not necessarily shared by those around them. Transitioning people are experiencing their own fears as well, which can make it difficult to recognize and respond to the fears of their loved ones.

For a period of time, friends and family may find that the transitioning person can think and talk of little other than the transition process and what is happening to him or her. This will pass, but it tends to be a miserable time for those who have to listen and can certainly alienate all but the staunchest supporters of the trans person. I'm sure that there were many times that my friends were thinking, "If he tells me about that stupid shot one more time, there will definitely be some shooting and it won't be with a needle." We all survived, but it is something for the trans person to keep in mind. He or she does have a great deal of control over how relationships with others are maintained during this period.

My advice to trans people is to listen, listen and listen some more. Your friends and family need to be heard, they need to have their feelings and fears recognized and acknowledged by you and they need some down time, some time away from the transition. Go to a movie, go on a picnic, do something that demonstrates that you are still the person they love and that you have more to talk about than the five hairs that are sprouting from your chin. Believe it or not, those hairs are not the stuff of engaging conversations.

Does transitioning cause major personality changes?

I often get this question from those who are intimately involved with a transitioning person and who are afraid of who or what this person will become. My answer to the question is "Maybe." I believe that a person's core personality will probably not change. The horror stories that female partners of transmen have heard about hormones are usually just that—stories. Although some transmen profess to feel more aggressive during certain times when the hormone levels peak in their bodies, many say that they feel calmer and more in control after they are free from the monthly estrogen-induced mood swings. It is highly unlikely that hormones alone will turn a kind, mild-mannered and monogamous individual into an abusive, rage-filled and cheating partner. In fact, most people tend toward just the opposite. Comfort with one's body and with the way one is seen by and treated by the world can have extremely positive effects. Most trans people, after transition, are happier, more fulfilled and easier to get along with.

That said, there can be certain problems. Testosterone can substantially increase the sex drive and, although a faithful partner will usually remain just that, the increase in sexual desire can be exhausting to some female partners. Wait it out. It will level off. Also, sometimes trans people do seem to change because they are finally becoming who they have always wanted and needed to be. Transitioning is a growth process and growth involves change. Some relationships do not survive it. Others thrive on it. Some couples grow apart, others grow closer. This happens in any relationship, whether it involves a gender transition or not, and, like any relationship, it is most important to keep the lines of communication open, to be willing to listen and to be as open and honest as possible.

What is the best way to show support for a trans person who is my friend, family member or partner?

The best way to show support for anyone, trans or not, is to find out who that person is and accept it. In the case of a trans person, acceptance means using the name the person has chosen, the correct pronoun ("he" for FtMs, "she" for MtFs), the correct references ("brother" for an FtM sibling, "son" for an FtM child) and respecting that person's wishes with regard to how, or if, he or she wants others to know about the transition. Transition is a scary time for everyone involved and a transitioning person is going through a lot. Try to be patient and realize that any major disruptions are temporary. However, remember that you have feelings, wants and needs that also have to be met and that you deserve an equal amount of respect and understanding. Subjugating your own needs and desires for too long a time can lead to bitterness and resentment, which, in turn, can destroy whatever relationship you have with the trans person. If the trans person is a partner or family member, counseling might be indicated and can be very beneficial. But the most important thing is to be there for that person and to let the person know that you want, and expect, him or her to be there for you.

What is the best way to show support for a trans person I don't know?

If you recognize that someone (a store clerk, an auto mechanic, a doctor) is transsexual while you are interacting with that person and you want to let the person know that you accept him or her, or that you support trans people in general, the best thing that you can do is nothing at all. Treat that person as you would treat anyone else in that position. Don't make an issue of it, don't wink or nod or make a comment that might reveal that person's status to anyone else. If the person is obviously trans, he or she is usually aware that it is obvious and will respect and appreciate you very much if you transact your business as you would with anyone else. He or she will be aware of your support and acceptance by what you *don't* say or do.

How can I learn to use the right name and pronouns?

There is nothing more annoying, and sometimes downright hurtful, to a transsexual person than the incorrect use of a name or pronoun. In the beginning of a transition, it is very difficult to make the switch and you will sometimes slip up. But, if you continue to use the pronoun "she" long after a transman has grown a full beard or if you continue to refer to Nancy as Ned several years after she has transitioned, you are in danger of completely alienating that person (if you haven't done so already). Your friendship or relationship is at stake and only you can decide if you value it enough to make the necessary changes in your thought processes.

What I have found, in questioning my friends and coworkers who easily made the adjustment and those who did not (and are still having trouble), is that those who were able to make the switch with little problem had made the decision to see me as an entirely different person—a male. One coworker said that she pretended that I was my own brother and she never made a mistake with my name or my pronoun. Those who constantly slip up, even after five years, are those who decided that I was a female that they would now have to refer to as "he" and "him." Even though I have a mustache and a goatee, no breasts, wear male clothing and am referred to as "he" by everyone else in the world, these few people continue to use the female pronoun.

They have not been able to make the switch. My only revenge is that they look like fools in public when they use "she" to refer to me and no one else knows who they are talking about. I can always roll my eyes, shake my head and give the waiter or sales clerk a secret smile to let him know how sorry I feel for someone who can't tell a man from a woman.

In all seriousness, however, to be unable to make this change signifies a lack of respect for your trans friend or loved one. I forgive children and, usually, parents, for who the transition may be so traumatic that it is impossible for them to fully adjust. I am less patient with friends and coworkers. When I hear such things as, "Oh, I'll never get that pronoun right," what it says to me is that you have no intention of trying, that you don't care enough for me to even make the effort. When I hear, "You'll always be female to me," what it says is that you have no idea who I really am and that you couldn't care less. With the limited amount of time I have on earth, why would I choose to spend it with someone who doesn't want to know or acknowledge who I am?

Can trans people successfully transition on the job? How is it done?

It would take a book to cover all the aspects of an on-the-job transition and, in fact, there have been books written about it, so I will just review the basics. It is important for a trans person to come up with a plan that he or she can present to an employer. That plan should include the following: how and when coworkers and clients will be told, a plan for resolving any bathroom issues that might arise, what time off will be needed and when, a time frame for name change, wardrobe change and change of pronoun usage, as well as a time frame for visible physical changes, if they will affect the trans person's interaction with others (clients, for example). The plan should be flexible and should be reworked, if necessary, with the employer's input.

It might sound like an invasion of a trans person's privacy to have to be so detailed, but, in most states, there are no protections at all for trans people and they can be easily fired with no recourse. Because of this, it is important for the trans person to make this transition as easy as possible for the employer. With a plan already in place, the employer does not have to worry about details. The employer should be assured that business will continue as usual and the trans person should make every effort to cause as little disruption as possible to the work environment.

This is not a time to make demands. Just as no one demands vacation or a raise, the trans person is not in any position to make demands of an employer during transition. Jobs are hard to come by. So are good employees. If both sides can be flexible, an on-the-job transition will go smoothly and successfully.

Trans people should be aware, however, that there are some states or cities (very few) in which they are protected. They should also be aware that certain questions or actions are illegal, no matter what. Trans people are under no obligation to discuss their surgeries or their genitalia. Sick leave is sick leave and, if a note from a doctor is required, the doctor performing a surgery can write a generic letter. No trans person should be questioned about his or her genitalia. The only concerns involved in a transition should be whether or not anything will affect the trans person's ability to do his or her job. Trans people who feel that their employer has acted illegally should contact an attorney or a legal assistance program.

Why should I have to share a bathroom at work with a trans person? It's a violation of my privacy.

There are actually those who believe that trans people use the restroom in order to spy on others or to get some kind of sexual thrill. How many sexy bathrooms have you actually been in lately? The bathroom issue is huge and seems to be a primary cause of strife in the workplace for trans and non-trans people alike. What most non-trans people don't realize is that the bathroom can be a terribly frightening place for trans people and they usually want to get in, take care of business and get out as quickly as possible. They have no interest in seeing or hearing what you are doing and they would rather not have you see or hear what they are doing. Most trans people, especially those who are new to transition, would prefer not to use public restrooms at all. I have known trans people who have refused liquid all day in order to avoid the restroom. Trust me when I say that we are there for one purpose only, just like you are, and that we have no ulterior motives.

Why are there more male-to-female transsexuals than there are female-to-male transsexuals?

There aren't. Recent statistics have shown that the numbers are about equal. However, there are several reasons why it *appears* that there are more MtFs than FtMs.

First of all, statistics about the number of transsexual people in existence have historically been gathered by psychiatrists, physicians and surgeons who work with trans populations by providing therapy, hormones and surgery. It is far easier for a female to live in society as a male without any hormones or surgery than vice versa. In the past and, probably still, many transgendered females have opted to do this rather than seek help through therapeutic and medical intervention. Therefore, they have not come to the attention of statistics gatherers.

Second, it is far easier for a transgendered female to live as a masculine female, dressing in men's clothing, wearing a male hairstyle and generally presenting in a masculine way than it is for a male to wear a dress, high heels and a wig.

Masculine females are far more accepted in our culture than feminine males. Therefore, some transgendered females have chosen to remain in a female role with the accoutrements of masculinity rather than undergo hormone treatments and surgeries, which always have risk. Transgendered males, on the other hand, are not allowed such a "luxury," so have transitioned instead.

Third, it has only been recently that transgendered females have had transsexual female-to-male role models to follow and emulate. Christine Jorgensen and Renee Richards were early and well-known male-to-female pioneers who provided models for other MtFs to follow. Now that there are visible FtM transsexuals in the media and elsewhere, transgendered females are aware of what is available for them and are beginning to take advantage of their options.

Also, testosterone is a very powerful hormone that overcomes estrogen quickly, making it easy for FtMs to assimilate rapidly into mainstream male society. FtMs are usually unrecognizable as such on the street. Beards, low voices, male pattern baldness and muscle increases all serve to create a presentation that is decidedly and unmistakably male. This ease of assimilation makes it very tempting for transmen to leave their pasts behind and to cease to identify as transsexual at all. Their new neighbors and friends don't know. If anything, FtMs appear as shorter-than-average males, but I have found that there are so many non-trans males who are shorter than I am (at 5' 7") that even that is not an issue.

MtFs have a more difficult time with assimilation. They are often much taller than the average female, with a much larger build and larger hands. Facial hair is often noticeable and electrolysis is time-consuming and expensive. The shape and size of the skull are sometimes issues. Vocal cords are lengthened by testosterone, but, once elongated, they do not shrink up, even under the influence of estrogen, so MtFs must work hard to master a higher-pitched voice or have surgery to alter it. For those with very low voices, it can be difficult. Although countless MtFs have successfully assimilated into mainstream female society, it can be a much more complex and tedious process than it is for FtMs. Because of these difficulties, more MtFs make use of resources, such as gender centers and support groups, than do FtMs, who tend to make use of resources for initial support, then disappear into the mainstream once the testosterone works its magic. But the women get even, because FtM surgery is far more expensive and the results are less satisfactory.

Socialization is also an issue. Men are socialized to speak out, to be visible and to press for what they need. Women are taught just the opposite. That socialization often carries over after transition, making MtFs more vocal and open about who they are and what they require, and, therefore, more visible in society than FtMs.

Things are changing, however. The Internet has been a boon for all trans people, bringing them information that was once not available. More and more FtMs are coming out and making their voices heard, becoming role models for transgendered females seeking gender reassignment. More doctors and surgeons are becoming aware of FtMs and are tailoring their practices toward these individuals, making FtM gender reassignment more accessible. Many transmen, however, are still in female-dominated occupations that are traditionally lower paying. Many are raising children without benefit of child support. And genital surgery, though vastly improved and more available in recent years, is still beyond the financial means of the majority of transmen. But we are out there and our voices will increase and continue. Look for us.

What do you think is the biggest hurdle facing trans people today?

Lack of visibility. Society's attitudes are a problem and I have just spent an entire book talking about that, but society's attitudes will not be changed until trans people are able to show themselves, talk about themselves and let others know who they are and what they need. It is definitely a circle—society won't change unless trans people come out and trans people won't come out unless society changes. Living openly as a transsexual carries a great deal of risk. Since there are no laws to protect us in most places, we stand to lose jobs, housing, medical insurance (not for gender transition—we don't have that now—but for routine medical care and illnesses that we get just like other people do) and a host of other basic rights. We also risk our personal safety. But these things will never improve until society is able to see us as we are—human beings (and taxpayers), like everyone else.

I have spoken to hundreds of college and university students and have heard pretty much the same thing with every class. Before they met me, they were afraid. Some of them hesitated to come to class on the day that I was presenting. They thought that I would be a freak or a monster. Instead, they were surprised (and relieved) to find out that I am "normal." They left class with a great deal of information and, hopefully, a different attitude. The only way that this kind of change can occur is when trans people are willing to be visible and to educate others. I understand why some cannot. They are supporting families and can't risk the loss of a job. They live in a rural or conservative area where their safety or their lives could be put in jeopardy. But those who can, should. And, to put a new spin on an old cliché, those who can, teach. We need to be engaged in open, educational dialogue with others whenever possible. And then we need to take a break, put up our feet and enjoy our lives.

Didn't answer your question? Want more information? Contact me at FtMatt@aol.com.